✻ Birmingham 25th nov 1995

Dedicated to a great friend. I hope you will apreciate it as much as I'm pleased to give it to you. Each time you will read it I want you to think about me. Make sure you don't forget about our friendship event when you will be ready to look for your eternal partner.

Merry Christmas with love and hapiness.

Leon

THE GHANAIAN REVOLUTION

THE GHANAIAN

REVOLUTION

Joseph G. Amamoo

Jafint Co., Publishers,
51 Prout Grove, London NW10, England

First published in 1988 by
JAFINT COMPANY, 51 Prout Grove,
London NW10, England

© Joseph G Amamoo 1988
ISBN 1 85421 016 5

Designed and produced by The SPA Limited,
Upton-upon-Severn, Worcestershire WR8 4HU
and printed and bound in Great Britain by
Billings & Son., Worcester, England

Dedicated with love to S. and S.

Preface

Ghana, since Independence in March 1957, has gone through two and a half coups. There was the first coup of February 1966, which toppled the Nkrumah régime. Next came the short-lived abortive coup of April 1967, whose duration was only a matter of a few hours. Then came the Acheampong coup of January 1972. In all three cases, the Government of the day was dislodged and replaced by a new one. To the extent that these two and a half coups disrupted the constitutional life of Ghana, they merit some study. For the events which followed them, more than the causes of these coups themselves, have had a profound influence on the course of political life in Ghana. Yet these coups, looked at retrospectively, did not produce major fundamental changes in the political, economic and social life of the Republic of Ghana. It was the rebellion-coup of June 4 1979 which can legitimately claim to have been a real revolution. For the historic event of June 4 1979 was indeed a revolution, in that it caused major fundamental changes in the body politic of Ghana. Unlike its predecessors, the June 4 1979 Revolution has left lasting and permanent effects on the course of Ghana history.

The story of the events before that date and the events which followed is the subject of this book. In telling the story, I have tried to give the necessary background which would be needed by a local reader, and more so by a foreign one, to appreciate fully the significance in Ghana's history of the Revolution of June 1979. For without such a background, the whole story would be truncated, even for a local Ghanaian reader.

The book, therefore, is divided into three sections. The first part deals with the historic background to the events of June 1979. The second part deals with the Revolution itself. Finally, the third part of the book deals with the immediate and probable future effects of the Revolution on Ghana and her people. This portion of the book is probably the most important one; for when all is said and done, when eventually the dust has settled, what is important for the country is not so much what has happened but what is yet to happen, or may happen. The June 4 Revolution is ultimately of historic interest only to the extent that it helps Ghanaians to avoid the mistakes of the past, so that the Ghana Revolution of 1979 would be, like the French Revolution of 1789, the American Revolution of 1776, and the Russian Revolution of 1917, a first and last revolution.

The question is often asked by many friends and well-wishers of Ghana: Why is it that Ghana, the first African colony to achieve Independence (peacefully and without bloodshed) should, since that historic event, have plunged into such a quagmire of political and economic chaos to the extent that currently the country is practically bankrupt? Why? I have attempted in this book to answer that question to the best of my ability. What has led the country which, in the mid-1950s, was one of the richest in Africa, to be now one of the poorest? I hope that the analysis which I offer in this book about the Ghana malaise is not only correct, but also helpful to us all, whatever our political affiliations, to reverse the current political trend towards bankruptcy, uncertainty and doom in Ghana.

In any case, even if the analysis, comments and views expressed in this book about the Ghana Revolution are not completely acceptable, if they lead to a mushrooming of more and better ideas about how to steer the country off the dangerous paths of the past to a more glorious and happier future, something useful would have been achieved.

To some extent, writing this book has not proved easy. For it involved commenting and pontificating on events which are still fresh in the public mind. In doing so, one is bound to tread on the toes of friends and even relations; but that is unavoidable. However dispassionate one tries to be, it is humanly impossible to remove completely the human element from the exercise which I have undertaken here. However, I have attempted to lessen the blows as much as possible by not publicly identifying certain persons who, either as participants in the Revolution or as victims, have played fairly significant roles in the whole national drama. It is in the interests of all concerned that their identities, in their life time, should be kept private.

Ghana, like all countries, has her full complement of armchair critics and theoreticians who, considering politics a dirty game, do not want to soil their beautiful hands, but are only too ready to criticise cynically every government action. Admittedly, although the activities of such people can frequently be irritating to those in public office, such criticisms have a very useful role to play in the proper development of a country such as Ghana. Even more important than the criticisms themselves is the need to offer proper valid alternatives to the public policies which one deprecates. I have tried to do so in the latter chapters of this book.

I have endeavoured while the events are still fresh in the public mind, to put the record straight, before the dust of history thickens on them, making them liable to all sorts of interpretations and disputations by persons who, although blessed with the benefit of detachment which history offers, would be devoid of the vibrant spirit of the period when the events took place.

My sources of information have chiefly been the local newspapers, especially the *Daily Graphic, Ghanaian Times,* the *Mirror,* the *People's Evening News, The Echo,* and *Punch.* The

11

various talks which I held with various military and civilian people of all walks of life have also been useful. This invaluable source of information reflects more accurately the true state of public opinion than would be gathered from the usual government press releases and statements. For the events in June 1979 gave positive proof to the veracity of most of the statements which, before 1979 were considered merely rumours. The reason is fairly simple. In pre-Revolutionary Ghana, with the massive suppression of human rights and the press, the only safe and proper way of getting the truth across to the public was in the form of rumours. As such, rumours in a developing country like Ghana cannot be scoffed at. For tomorrow's "fact" is today's "rumour".

I have also quoted from Government publications where necessary to show, again and again, that the régimes before June 1979 were condemned invariably from their own lips and by their own handiwork.

Fortunately for me, in this work there have been few books by experts on Ghana to work on. For due to the repressive political climate of the 1970s in Ghana, intellectual work has not flourished. For how can dispassionate, intellectual work be carried out, when its probable end result would be a long spell in prison without trial, in conditions reminiscent of British jails of the 19th century? The dearth of other books on the current political period means that I have been able to approach my assignment with the independence of mind and detachment which a spell in prison (without trial) has rejuvenated and kept alive.

Yet, when all is said and done, "no man is an island, entire of itself". Indeed not. And I would be rather ungrateful if I did not mention here a few good friends from whom I have gained immensely in knowledge. The Roman Catholic Bishop of Accra, His Grace Dr Andoh, a saintly man and one really dedicated to the spiritual and material upliftment of all Ghanaians, of whatever political or religious persuasion, would always be to me one of the best examples of the modern Ghanaian churchman, as he tries to grapple with the spiritual, moral and economic problems besetting his flock. Nor can one forget or ignore the American, Father Quechmore, and the Ghanaian Father H Senoo; stalwart and fearless aides and colleagues of the Bishop, who in spite of immense difficulties and at a time when they ran tremendous personal risks, stood up for human rights and moderation in Ghana.

To my wife and daughters, I am indebted for their continued interest in this work, and for all the help and assistance which they have given me. This work would have been impossible without their love, support and help.

J.G. Amamoo

Chapter 1 – Setting the Scene

Although the roots of the Revolution of 1979 can be traced to the coup of 1972, it is essential that the appropriate background is provided here before one launches into the events themselves.

On 6 March 1957, Ghana, then known as the Gold Coast, became the first country in colonial Africa to achieve Independence. This historic event was of tremendous importance not only to Ghana, but also for the rest of Africa. Under the leadership of Dr Kwame Nkrumah, Ghana had achieved independence after 113 years of British colonial rule. Following independence, Dr Nkrumah vigorously set about a massive and rapid development of the country. Impressive achievements were chalked up, especially in the fields of education. Hundreds of secondary schools were opened, and elementary schools were started in villages which previously had never seen any. Also to help the illiterate masses (about 80% of the population) a mass-education programme was launched nationwide. The fervour and enthusiasm which this mass-education campaign generated was so infectious that soon, thousands of old villagers had taken to reading and writing basic English and some of the local languages. The experiment became so popular that other African countries, including Nigeria and Sierra Leone, sent people to Ghana to learn of the great success in adult education which was taking place.

In addition to all this, thousands of scholarships were granted to Ghanaian students for courses such as medicine, engineering, architecture, law, vocational studies, business and commerce. These scholarships were not available only in the traditional

Western countries, such as Britain or the U.S. For the first time, Ghanaian students could go to the Eastern European countries, and China. Some of the scholarships were even awarded to African students from countries which were not yet independent then, such as Nigeria, Kenya, and other African countries.

The Nkrumah régime during the period that it was in office launched a gigantic programme of industrialisation. For the first time in the country's history, a chocolate factory was set up in Tema, a port town near Accra. This was long overdue, since Ghana, the world's leading cocoa-producer, had till then exported all her cocoa, only to import chocolates from overseas at very exhorbitant prices. In the industrialisation programme the following factories were among the many which were set up: a tomato-processing factory in the north; a ceramic factory near Saltpond, on the coast; wood-processing factories in Ashanti and the Western and Eastern Regions: a gold refining factory in Tarkwa; and a shoe and bag making factory in Kumasi, capital of Ashanti.

In the field of communications, a wide network of motor roads was set up quickly in the country, stretching to various parts of Ghana, where until then people were forced to walk on bush paths in order to travel from one village to another. This improvement in the communication system also led to better transportation of food from the rural areas to the urban centres.

Post offices and telephones began to appear in small villages and towns which previously had not seen any. Ghana's only harbour then, Takoradi Harbour, which had been built in 1925 under the British colonial administration, was expanded. In addition to this, a new harbour was built at Tema, near Accra, to facilitate the export of Ghana's main produce, namely cocoa, timber, gold, manganese, diamonds and bauxite. The new harbour was joined to the capital by a first-class dual carriageway of about 18 miles, which eased the congestion on the old Accra-Tema coastal road. The latter was an old road, which passes through a congested, over-crowded part of Accra, consequently causing a rather high motor accident rate.

Ghana's chief export, cocoa, which accounts for about 70 per cent of her foreign exchange earnings was given a big boost. The local price which was paid to the local farmers in local currency was raised in order to induce them to grow more cocoa. Further assistance to the farmers was given in the form of heavily subsidised fertilisers, high-yield seedlings, and the provision of a mass cocoa-spraying campaign.

Around this period, a virus disease of the cocoa-tree was found to be developing rapidly. The only cure was to cut off the diseased trees and spray the healthy ones. Through a massive education campaign aimed at the farming communities, the cutting-out programme, which they had violently resisted when it had been launched by the colonial administration in 1946, was now accepted. Over £1 million was allocated to the country's cocoa research centre, known as WACRI (West African Cocoa Research Institute) in order to help it to expand its activities and develop new varieties of cocoa, more resistant to the disease.

Furthermore, the Nkrumah régime made serious efforts to diversify the agricultural infra-structure of the country, by encouraging the development and growth of other cash crops such as sisal, fruit, cotton, palm trees and rice. For long before the advent of cocoa in Ghana in 1879 from Fernardo Po, the palm tree was the chief source of the country's export earnings. The tree provided palm oil which was used in the soap and chemical industries. Other by-products of the tree included palm wine (a sweet, mildly alcoholic beverage), a local gin, popularly known as *Akpeteshie,* which is distilled from palm wine; palm kernel, for heating and cooking purposes. Even the trunk of the tree was used as a cheap source of fuel in the villages.

Dr Nkrumah, after a long spell in the USA as a student of

political science and theology, had returned home in 1947 with a determination not only to get freedom and independence for his country, but also to lay the foundations for a great economic development, which would make Ghana a shining example to the rest of Africa. He threw himself body and soul into his avowed programme of political independence for his country, with demonic enthusiasm and determination, and by 6 March 1957, he could triumphantly show his people that he had delivered the goods. With the same verve and energy he waded into the problem of creating a modern industrial nation from an undeveloped, but potentially rich country.

To ensure rapid industrialisation of the country, he established the Industrial Development Corporation (IDC). The corporation was empowered to:

(a) Carry on all activities in connection with the development of industry, including the making of industrial products.

(b) Promote such activities by other bodies or persons and to promote the establishment or expansion of other bodies to carry on such activities either independently or under the control or partial control of the corporation, to give assistance, including financial assistance by the taking up of share or loan capital to such bodies or persons.

(c) to carry on such activities in association with other bodies or persons (including Government activities or local government authorities) or as managing agents or otherwise on their behalf. £4 million was set up as working capital for the corporation. Other boards such as the National Food Board, Agricultural Produce Marketing Board, State Gold Mining Corporation, the Diamond Marketing Board etc. were set up. They were

18

all designed to permeate the various aspects of the industrial and economic spheres of the country, and to ensure that as rapidly as possible Ghana became an industrialised country. The aim was that primarily the country should be able to drastically cut her vast imports of foreign, manufactured items, and secondarily, be in the position to export some of her manufactured goods to surrounding African states, which may need them.

Towards this end, a major achievement of the period was the construction of the multi-million Akosombo Project, about 90 miles from Accra. Built chiefly with American money and British assistance, the Akosombo project involved the creation of a completely new township, a new harbour (Tema), a hydro-electric dam, and the production of electricity for the country. Indeed, although primarily the purpose of the project was to ensure the supply of cheap electricity for the processing of bauxite into aluminium, the surplus electricity is being sold to surrounding African states, e.g. Togo. The project has made an immense contribution to the industrial development of the country by providing jobs, housing for the employees of the firms which are based on and operate around the project. It has also helped Ghanaians to acquire skills in modern technology, which would not otherwise have been easily available. Although the Master-Agreement between the American firm and the Nkrumah régime by which the project came into being has often been criticised as being unfair to Ghana, it must be borne in mind that at the time of the Agreement, the Nkrumah régime, not having the requisite financial or technical resources to launch the programme single-handed, was not in a very strong bargaining position.

In order to encourage foreign investors into the country, the Government offered liberal investment terms, including up to five years 'tax-holiday' to pioneer investors, and also assurances that despite the avowed socialist policies of the government, foreign enterprises would not be nationalised. Furthermore, the Government committed itself publicly to the payment of fair and adequate compensation should the need arise, in the public interest, for any nationalisation. Indeed statements by Dr Nkrumah in the early pre-independence period showed a determination to utilise both *capitalism* and *socialism* to the benefit of Ghana. Speaking on capital investment in the Legislative Assembly (Parliament) on March 1, 1954, Dr Nkrumah had this to say: "I am confident that with goodwill and understanding, Government and private enterprise can combine to attain our objective of progressive industrial development".

In the field of public health, the Nkrumah régime undertook the construction of major hospitals in the regional capitals, while modest-sized clinics were built in the smaller towns and villages. The rural clinics and dispensaries were of particular importance, since they brought the benefits of modern medicine, however insufficient and limited, to areas that till then were perpetually victims of such tropical diseases as amoebic dysentery, smallpox, yaws, leprosy, typhoid fever, and craw-craw. Nationwide campaigns were launched to educate the illiterate on basic hygiene and health, and the need to report illnesses at the earliest possible opportunity to the nearest clinic or hospital, instead of first spending much money and time frequenting the homes of local juju-men and herbalists whose treatment sometimes turned out to be more dangerous than efficacious. Although, before the advent of modern medicine the people had no alternative but to rely on the juju-men and women, the direct and dramatic results which modern nedicine provided, especially in the treatment of tropical diseases, showed conclusively that modern medicine, where available, was superior to its predecessor. The trouble was that modern medicine was not available to vast numbers of the population.

Mention should here be made of the tremendous contribution which has been made by the Roman Catholic and Protestant missions in the field of public health. By establishing clinics and hospitals in remote areas, where the Government has been unable to do so, these missions have helped greatly to raise the level of health of the people of Ghana. Recently, the Ahmadiya Movement has also started to provide health facilities in a few towns.

To continue with the brief outline of the achievements of the Nkrumah régime, right from the onset Dr Nkrumah emphasised the need for Ghana to assist in the liberation of other African states. As such, following Independence on 6 March 1957 he threw himself, body and soul, into the African liberation movement. Having suffered at first hand racial discrimination and insults in the USA where he was for many years a student and teacher, he was determined to ensure that the black man regained his self-respect wherever he might be, and that at least in Africa, the black man's home, there should be no discrimination against him. His conviction and enthusiasm inspired millions of Ghanaians, educated or illiterate, who felt the same. It would be irrational and dishonest for any Ghanaian now, with the aid of hindsight, and especially following some of the disclosures of the unsavoury acts of the Nkrumah régime after its fall, to state that Nkrumah's African policy did not have the fullest support of practically the whole population.

The Pan-African policy of Nrumah, envisaged not only the liberation of the rest of colonial Africa, but also the unity of the continent on the lines of the USA. To the millions of people in Africa who were still not free, Nkrumah became a liberator and emancipator. They looked up to him to effect the decolonisation of their own countries. They were not disappointed in their expectations. Firstly, the Nkrumah régime established a number

21

of embassies, high commissions and consulates in many parts of the world, especially in Africa, to project "the African personality" and to contribute to the psychological re-education of black people through a radical eradication of the "colonial mentality", whereby everything "colonial" or "white" was good, and all else was bad. By constantly harping on this and similar themes, Nkrumah became the idol of the black people in Africa, America, West Indies and Europe in the late 1940s and right through the 1960s. Soon Ghana became the Mecca for deprived African politicians, whose countries were struggling for independence. Conferences and major meetings on Africa and Africans were held in Ghana, all financed by the Ghana Government. And the Nkrumah régime drew happily to Accra many of the present generation of African leaders, who at that time were only deemed agitators or political trouble-makers in their own countries.

In addition to establishing embassies to carry across to Africa especially the message of freedom and justice, Nkrumah was prepared to back his word with Ghana's money. For what is the use of mere words of support and encouragement, not buttressed by the provision of funds, especially when most of the people who looked up to Nkrumah were engaged in both an ideological and a colonial-guerilla war with their foreign masters? Fortunately for these struggling non-independent African states, Ghana in the 1950s was a relatively wealthy country. Her cocoa, timber and mineral exports of gold diamonds, manganese and bauxite were booming. The world cocoa price was high, and the future looked very rosy. As such, substantial funds of Ghana were committed, both publicly and secretly, to the African liberation movement. Furthermore, Nkrumah never hesitated to assist black Americans who needed help towards projects which favoured the black man's liberation and enhancement. For he was convinced that Ghana had a historic duty to herself and to other black people, wherever they may be, to contribute to the upliftment and development of black people.

In short, it would be correct to state that the foreign policy objectives of Nkrumah had the support of practically the whole population of Ghana. At the mass rallies in towns and villages, Nkrumah's African programme was endorsed again and again with public enthusiasm approaching hysteria. The local newspapers, radio, and later television; local politicians, academics, students and even political opponents of Nkrumah agreed and supported the African liberation programme. At that time it was not a question of Capitalism v Socialism. It was simply a question of: "Do you support the liberation and independence of other African countries which are still not free?" To all rational people, including those in the villages, once the issues were explained to them in the local vernacular, the answer was plain and obvious.

Right from the arrival of Nkrumah in Ghana in 1947, the whole movement had been geared towards politics as a means for achieving political independence first for Ghana and secondly, for the rest of Africa. As such, economics and economic issues took only a secondary position. On this paramount issue of political independence, even Nkrumah's political opponents had no room to dissociate themselves from him without committing political suicide or appearing to be traitors not only to their country, but to the whole black race.

Paraphrasing the Bible, Nkrumah repeatedly emphasised the need to: "seek first the political kingdom, and all other things shall be added unto you". Thus it was politics all the way. And many of the prominent Ghana leaders, present and past, who subsequently broke away from Nkrumah, e.g. Dr J.B. Danquah, Mr Obetsebi-Lamptey, Kwesi Lamptey, Victor Owusu, K.A. Gbedemah and others, did so not over the Ghana-

Africa independence issue, but over internal strategy, bribery and corruption, trends towards dictatorship, communism, and a growing proclivity towards one-man rule in the late 1950s and early 1960s.

Whatever may be the criticisms of the economic and internal policies which were pursued by Nkrumah, especially towards the latter stages of his rule, his foreign policy and its achievements were fully supported by the people of Ghana, and many black people outside. Furthermore the non-Ghanaian African supporters of Nkrumah's foreign policy benefited psychologically and sometimes financially from the implementation of this policy.

On the economic front, the achievements of the Nkrumah régime were impressive, although not as much as in the field of foreign affairs. Apart from concrete achievements which can be measured in material terms, such as the number of schools and colleges built, the mileage of roads constructed, the number of hospitals and small town clinics built, the new factories erected, the whole period ushered in an era of enthusiasm, progress and development which continued vigorously right on to the last days.

Chapter 2 – Counting the Cost

As stated in the previous chapter, the Nkrumah régime made definite and positive achievements in the field of foreign affairs and politics, by gaining independence for the country in March 1957. In Ghana's economic and social development there were some clear achievements. However, it is only rational to assess the cost to the nation of these remarkable achievements in order to evaluate their cost-benefit to the people of Ghana.

Late in 1963, the Nkrumah régime had belatedly come to a conclusion that it had overstretched itself in the field of, for example, foreign affairs. It began to implement a policy of closing some of the embassies. But this was not easy, since every closure of an embassy meant depriving quite a few persons of their comfortable jobs, and also shrinking the foreign affairs "empire". Human nature being what it is, nobody is ever keen to preside over the diminution of his own empire or field of influence, however justified in the national interest such a course of action might be.

Although Ghana, a recipient of aid from richer countries, was morally justified in giving aid to less developed African states, the fact still remains that Ghana's excessive loans and aid to some of these nations cannot be justified considering Ghana's own dire needs, even at the height of her affluence in the 1950s.

The régime should have concentrated more on making Ghana a show-case of African development, rather than frittering away the country's meagre resources on a gigantic effort to help all Africa, noble though such an objective may have been.

The trouble was that in his whole approach to the problems of

Ghana's role in Africa, Nkrumah had always warring in him his "Trotsky" and his "Stalin". The question was whether to export Ghana's freedom and independence or not to do so, but rather concentrate on Ghana's own development. Nkrumah's Trotsky-ism won through from 1957 to February 1966, when he was toppled from office. Naturally a heavy price had to be paid by Ghana for exporting her revolution to other parts of Africa.

Apart from the tremendous expenditure on embassies and consulates, there was also immense financial contribution to the various liberation movements in Africa in the 1950s and 60s. By the very nature of the whole exercise such transfers of money had to be very secret. However, long before Nkrumah's fall, there was the general belief that some of the funds destined for the liberation movements were not reaching their destination, and that somehow, en route, some of them ended in the coffers and bank accounts of the emissaries. Even while the struggle continued unabated, certain "revolutionaries" did not fail to cash in financially on the situation.

It is, however, in the field of Ghana's own economic and political development that the country paid the heaviest price in terms of human and financial resources for the policies and actions of Nkrumah. The causes for the failures in these fields are attributable to the following:

1. A general disinterest in economic matters, as opposed to political matters, by the leader himself.
2. Over-hasty economic planning.
3. Lack of proper supervision of the Government by Nkrumah himself, and
4. The lack of due emphasis on agriculture.

Let us now attempt to analyse these faults and weaknesses of the régime in greater detail.

1. Nkrumah's Disinterest in economic matters

Throughout the campaign for political independence, Nkrumah had emphasised the need to seek first the political kingdom. The argument was that after the political kingdom had been achieved, economic independence would follow. This initially made sense, for without full political control over its own affairs, it is difficult to see how a small developing country such as Ghana could undertake a proper and effective control and direction over its economy. The local retail trade was predominantly controlled by Lebanese and Indian nationals, while the export trade in the country's chief foreign exchange earners, namely cocoa, timber, gold, diamonds, manganese and bauxite were in the hands of British firms.

Nkrumah was essentially a politician. Consequently, after the achievement of Ghana's independence on 6 March 1957, he turned his attention not to the pursuit of the economic kingdom for Ghana, but the pursuit of the political kingdom for other African states. At dawn on 6 March 1957, as the Union Jack was unfurled in a colourful ceremony at Accra to usher in the independence of the Gold Coast, and the birth of Ghana, Nkrumah's first statement to the excited, vast crowd present had been: "The Independence of Ghana is meaningless unless followed by the liberation and independence of the rest of Africa".

It would be idle and unfair to suggest that Nkrumah did not pay any attention to economic affairs. Of course he did. But it was palpably obvious to any serious observer of Ghana affairs that the leader's main interest, and first love, was African liberation and African affairs. Thus although periodically public, lip service was paid to the needs of the economy, on the whole, the running of the country's economy was left in other hands. On occasions, he took up the responsibility for economic planning, only to relegate it to other ministers, as he got more and more engrossed in African affairs.

Furthermore, this major interest and involvement in African liberation had a profound shift in his foreign policy and economic policy. For although whether Nkrumah was a communist or not had never been satisfactorily resolved, even by the Watson Commission (a Royal Commission from Britain which had been appointed in 1949 under the chairmanship of Mr Watson) to enquire into the Gold Coast riots and political disturbances, it can be stated, without fear of contradiction that in his earlier policy statements before and after Independence, Nkrumah tried to be non-aligned as much as possible, in the ideological war between the East and the West. He opened embassies in the East to counter-balance those already opened in the West. He encouraged local private enterprise, and foreign Western investment, while simultaneously opening Ghana's doors to economic aid and assistance from the East.

The fact still remains that a rapid and deep flirtation was developing with the East by Nkrumah, who had previously sprinkled many of his public statements with the success of the United States as a nation, and the freedom in that country. This continuous involvement with the East became more prominent from 1960, when Ghana became a republic in the Commonwealth, with Nkrumah as the first President. From then on, especially, Nkrumah's public statements shifted from being non-aligned to a pronounced anti-Western stance. On all the major African problems and issues which interested him – apartheid in South Africa, racial discrimination generally, colonialism in Africa (French, British or Belgian) and other major world issues including nuclear tests in Africa – Nkrumah saw the West as the enemy and the main stumbling block in the path of his policy of emancipating Africa from all forms of colonialism, be they economic or political. Although till his last days, he privately admired the quality of British goods and the British way of life, the political path which he had chosen was bound to bring him into direct or indirect confrontation with the West. In the immediate post-war international climate, the fierce East-West confrontation of the 1950s and 1960s, Nkrumah's publicly chosen and announced political path, could not but endear him and his country to the East at the expense of the West.

Numerous public statements at home and abroad began to castigate the West. Stringent articles and books poured forth strongly attacking the West, and openly advocating Marxist-Socialism as the panacea for Ghana's economic and political problems. From non-alignment initially in 1948-1959, Nkrumah had, by the mid 1960s, metamorphosed into a full-blown "Marxist" or "Communist" in all but name. This political metamorphosis became even more pronounced after a long, extensive tour of the Soviet Union and the rest of Eastern Europe and China in 1961. He returned to Ghana a completely changed man. The anti-Western attacks became less diplomatic and more open.

Now a few major snags began to develop. To begin with, although Nkrumah was openly committed to a pro-East policy, the country which he was leading, after 113 years of British colonial rule, had become so entrenched in the British way of life, politically, constitutionally, legally and in all other spheres of human endeavour, that short of a complete national rebirth and reincarnation, no leader – not even Nkrumah – could reverse the trend. The country's educational system from top to bottom, was modelled on the British system. Most of the text books, and even the hymn books were in English and were the same as those used in Britain. The educated, especially the heads of the Judiciary, Civil Service, Armed Forces, Corporations, were all trained in Britain, or in the Western tradition. Most of the private business men, politicians, journalists, lawyers and doctors were trained in Britain or the USA. Consequently, there was the awkward situation whereby the leader of the nation was openly advocating strong marxist-socialism, while the élite of the country, although publicly joining in the universal chorus, were privately holding entirely opposite views and ideas, generated by their upbringing.

This dichotomous attitude to public affairs was not confined to the categories mentioned above. Even some of the leading supporters of Nkrumah, at the height of his socialist advocacy, were publicly known to be engaged in vast scale business enterprises, acquisition of property on a grand scale, and the rapid building of impressive bank accounts both locally and abroad, either in their own names or through their wives, relatives and friends. Such unsocialist activities, to put it mildly, were known to the public, or at least strongly suspected. Subsequent events and the reports of the various Commissions of Enquiry which were set up to investigate the assets and properties of the Cabinet Ministers and other party officials of the Nkrumah régime and those of their wives, substantially confirmed as facts what previously had been rebutted as mere rumours.

It was a situation in which Nkrumah and a handful of his followers, out of conviction (e.g. Eric Heyman, Editor of the Evening News, T.D. Baffoe, Editor of the Ghanaian Times and a few others) were pulling in one direction, while the rest of the nation, despite publicly applauding Nkrumah's marxist statements and actions, were privately pulling in the other. The contradictions in the whole Nkrumah period continued to show themselves right up to the collapse of the régime in February 1966.

2. Over-hasty planning

Nkrumah was determined to industrialise the country quickly.

As such, development plan upon development plan was issued and publicised between 1959 and 1965. Advice from local and especially foreign experts was profusely sought. Some of the advice was bad, even disasatrous, and can be said to have been responsible for the final economic collapse of the régime. For often it did not appear to take into account local conditions and the fundamental conservative nature of the vast majority of the people of Ghana, even though in public, especially in the towns, they were hysterically applauding marxist policies and programmes. When it is remembered that about 80–85% of the population live in the rural areas, with their small, self-owned farms and smallholdings, it is difficult to believe how a fundamental change in the economic life and means of earning a livelihood of the vast section of the population could be achieved without a ruthless programme of collectivisation or nationalisation. This would have been violently resisted on all fronts, and would have led to more repression by the régime.

Due to over-hasty planning, the country's economy was overstretched. Many of the factories which were set up needed to import many items from abroad. For example, a tomato processing factory which was set up in the north had to import cases, chemical preservatives, machinery and spare parts. To cap it all, the tomato farms which were meant to feed the factory could not produce enough for the factory. Factories were sited in areas more for political considerations than on the grounds of cost-benefit to the nation. A gold refinery machine imported from the Soviet Union had a capacity far in excess of the gold production of Ghana. The machine has stayed idle to this day.

Anticipating a growth in the economy which, unfortunately, never materialised, an 18-mile motorway was built to join the new harbour Tema, and the capital Accra. Despite the millions of pounds spent on it, the road is very little used. The motor roads which were built in the period in the rural areas were necessary.

The 100 miles of extra railway line built by the régime were necessary. But a whole host of public buildings – excluding hospitals, clinics, colleges – cannot be justified if the net result of these expenditures was eventually to lead to the country's economic bankruptcy. Was it essential in a country where many people have no proper water to drink, or are twenty or thirty miles from the nearest hospital, to spend state funds erecting public statues of the leader, even before he was dead? Few intelligent people would justify such unessential expenditure. The few who do have obviously got their priorities wrong.

In a country where there is one doctor to about every 100,000 of the population, where infant mortality and malnutrition are still high on the list of killers of babies, where "Kwashiokor" is still a major national health problem, one has to think not twice, but many times, before supporting unessential expenditure.

When eventually the Nkrumah régime collapsed the commissions of enquiry which followed the demise of the régime established that in some cases, the costs of the projects and state purchases had been inflated, with the consequent loss to Ghana of millions of pounds. All this at a time when newly established factories were forced to close down for lack of foreign exchange to import essential raw materials or spare parts.

Since the June 1979 Revolution, it has become fashionable for certain politicians and students to advocate the execution of all those responsible for such and subsequent corruption or misappropriation of state funds in Ghana. I am of the view that, callous and heartless the actions of these people might have been, the appropriate punishment is to deprive them of their ill-gotten gains, and to sentence them, after a decent trial, to a reasonable period of imprisonment. It is true that as the Government was finding its feet there were bound to be mistakes, major and minor, both in planning and execution of projects. But some of the mistakes committed in the 1960s are difficult to excuse. Especially so when later evidence turned out from the commissions of enquiry that some of these projects had been executed probably because of the attractive unofficial commissions of 10% which the foreign firms and financiers involved were prepared to pay to the Ghanaian politicians concerned.

3. Lack of proper supervision of the Government

The bribery and corruption which some of these hastily executed projects produced was massive. Long before the coup of February 1966 which brought the régime to an end, it was well-known that a number of ministers and prominent party officials, who previously were people of modest means at best or sometimes, of rather limited means, had suddenly become very affluent. They and their wives, often had become not only opulent but also quite corpulent. The dramatic increase in girth, the sprouting of homes and buildings in top areas of Accra, the conspicuous display of affluence and wealth, in a land of poverty and deprivation, could not be explained in any other way but the obvious. For none of these persons were known publicly to be minting money, or to have inherited a fortune, or to have won the Pools, or Lotto. That some of the ministers and top party officials, although publicly singing the virtues of scientific socialism or marxist-socialism or Nkrumahism, or African socialism, were busily engaged in rampant, unashamed capitalism, was known to a lot of people, certainly to the intelligent ones, who were not blind. The commissions' reports confirmed mostly what had been known or suspected all the time.

The question has often been asked why the academics, intellectuals and others did not openly speak out against these criminal activities of some of the politicians of the period. The answer is simple. In a political climate where open criticism of the régime meant long bouts of imprisonment without trial, in very humiliating and degrading physical conditions, few people would blame all those who had courage to talk only after the régime's collapse!

Yet even in the difficult days of dictatorship and repression, stout-hearted men such as Dr J.B. Danquah, Obetsebi-Lamptey, Victor Owusu, Joe Appiah, Paa Willie, Kwesi Lamptey, Chief S.D. Dombo, to name only a few, had the courage to speak out against injustice, bribery and corruption, nepotism and dictatorship. They knew the risks which they were running in so doing, and were prepared to pay the price for their actions. The first two gentlemen died in Nkrumah's prisons, without any trial whatsoever. The others were among over 4,000 persons who spent long periods of imprisonment without trial in Nkrumah's jails. A few of them died after their release.

Since Nkrumah's fall, it has been argued ad infinitum, whether Nkrumah knew about the corrupt activities of some of his stalwart ministers and supporters. That he was aware of infractions of the law and moral standards by his men is incontrovertible. He was the leader and knew, or must have known about his ministers' criminal activities. Indeed, in a famous "Dawn Broadcast" on 8th April 1961 by Nkrumah himself, he strongly condemned, in full, the rampant bribery and corruption among the top echelons of the Government and party. Following this well-acclaimed speech, in September 1961 some of Nkrumah's most prominent ministers and party officials were dismissed and publicly disgraced. A few months later, without any public explanation whatsoever, some of these same persons who had been condemned by Nkrumah himself as corrupt, decadent and unfit for public office, were all reinstated, to the gross embarrassment of the politicians, students, academics, and intellectuals, who, naively, had sent him glowing congratulations when he originally dismissed these men!

Subsequently in February 1966, after the coup which brought the régime to an end, Mr J.W.K. Harlley, at a press conference, told the press and public that as head of Special Branch, he frequently gave Nkrumah details of the activities of his men and that Nkrumah kept the files on his ministers and used that information to keep them quiet and blackmail them. At the time he was speaking, Mr Harlley was Vice-Chairman of the Military Government which had replaced the Nkrumah régime. He was also the head of the country's Police Force.

A more charitable interpretation of Nkrumah's inability or unwillingness to check the corrupt, decadent activities of some of his ministers could be the preponderent time and interest he took in external affairs to the consequent lack of supervision and control over his ministers. As such, they were free to do what they liked, so long as they kept openly praising "Nkrumahism", scientific socialism, African socialism, and African Unity.

Even in this chaotic and messy state of affairs, when capitalism was denounced in public, and enthusiastically subscribed to in private, there are some of Nkrumah's ministers and top officials whose honesty, dedication and abhorrence of bribery and corruption were the redeeming features of a government whose public statements and private actions were becoming more and more contradictory. Among these may be mentioned, for the purposes of history and in the interests of fairness, the following persons: Dr W.C. Ekow-Daniels, Kwaku Boateng (Interior Minister), Kofi Baako (Defence Minister), E.K.Bensah, I.K. Chiebuah (Education Minister) and "the socialist boys" – Eric Heyman (Editor of the Evening News), T.D.Baffoe (Editor of the Ghanaian Times), Kofi Batsa, Kweku Akwei, Tawiah Adamafio (once the most powerful man in the country, after Nkrumah himself). These men courageously, right up to the end exposed and fought bribery

35

and corruption in their own field. Inspired by idealism and altruism, they followed Nkrumah faithfully, made no money out of the "struggle" and their period of discipleship, unlike some of their more corrupt colleagues. The commissions of enquiry completely exonerated them and established their honesty. These men could thus, with a clear conscience and clean hands, face their compatriots and gladly say – "We might have been wrong or too gullible, but at least we acted honestly and in truth". They, therefore, did not have to go through extreme anguish and mental torture as did some of their colleagues.

As to the question of whether Nkrumah himself was in any way involved in the corruption and bribery openly indulged in by his ministers before the coup of February 1966, the verdict should be "Not Proven", although this is very unlikely. Statements which were made by his own ministers and colleagues after his fall would suggest strongly that the ministers, at least some of them, knew of, or suspected his involvement in some of those practices. The speeches and statements of Krobo Edusei, Ayeh-Kumi, Halm, Kwaku Boateng and others before the Commissions of Enquiries (1966-67) speak for themselves, and implicate the President.

Were these men lying? Were they just saying something to extricate themselves or were they speaking the truth? Or were they shifting all blame on Nkrumah because the régime was dead, and the master was politically finished?

Why Nkrumah continued to have in his entourage persons whom he himself had publicly condemned as corrupt and ideologically bankrupt and not sufficiently socialist can never be explained, except by the man himself. Alas, he is dead. The present and future generations of Ghanaians would therefore only speculate on Nkrumah's reasons for his strange reaction to the criminal aberrations of some of his colleagues.

4. Lack of due emphasis on agriculture

Throughout the régime's period insufficient attention was paid to agriculture. Nkrumah's fervent desire was to effect rapid and early industrialisation of Ghana, with the successful industrialisation of the Soviet Union as a guideline. As such, although periodically lip-service was paid publicly to the need to diversify agriculture, the need to produce more crops apart from cocoa, on the whole not much was done or achieved on the agricultural front. This was a major mistake. For Ghana is an agricultural country, with about 80–85% of the people living on and off the land as farmers. The insufficient attention and funds devoted to agriculture meant that ultimately the country was spending heavily on imports of food, mostly from the Western countries. From about 1964, the economic facts began to catch up with the régime.

Cocoa production began to fall, just as the world price was also falling. Ghana, which at the time of Independence had foreign reserves of about £250 million, had to dig deeper and deeper into these reserves to finance food imports and the importation of medicines, machinery, spare parts etc., mostly from the West. As the reserves fell drastically, soon the position was reached when the country was experiencing enormous problems in its balance of payments. Both short and medium term foreign debts caused foreign lenders – mainly Western – to refuse to give further credit facilities to the régime which was rapidly going bankrupt. The country did not have money to pay for its imports, and credit was no longer available from the West.

The local factories, both state and private, thus began to grind to a halt, due to the insufficiency of raw materials and spare parts. Essential commodities such as sugar, milk, sardines, corned beef, rice began to run out, and people queueing for food began to appear in the country for the first time.

The public began to grumble privately, and sometimes openly, although generally they continued to praise African socialism, Nkrumah and scientific socialism. The numerous calls by the régime for belt-tightening were scoffed at, especially when such appeals were made at the very time some of the ministers and high party officials and supporters were building sumptuous houses, acquiring properties and businesses and rapidly loosening their own belts!

Consequences

Nkrumah's pavlovian reaction to these severe economic problems at home was to get more and more involved in international affairs, and to adopt a more violent anti-western stance and tone. Castigation of the West at every public meeting, local or abroad, became the order of the day. The state newspapers, the *Evening News* and *Ghanaian Times*, continued faithfully to urge the people to tighten their belts and work and pray for better days to come. Later the *Daily Graphic* (formerly owned by the British *Daily Mirror* group) was also acquired by the State. So was the *Ashanti Pioneer*, which was originally privately owned by Mr Tsiboe, but was subsequently censored, banned, and eventually compulsorily acquired by the State. Thus all the four papers in the country, plus the radio and television, joined in the same theme – praising the leader, the régime, and the exposition of the causes which were dear to Nkrumah's heart. Coupled with this went a violent repression of all opposition views and ideas and the character assassination of all those who opposed Nkrumah or the régime, or criticised them in any way. Former colleagues of Nkrumah, such as E.K. Dadson and others, who fell foul of the President, suddenly found themselves the targets of "spontaneous" mass demonstrations, as so-called CIA agents.

The opposition groups led originally by Dr J.B. Danquah continued to oppose Nkrumah's extreme left-wing rhetoric and actions. Using the only paper that then supported them, the *Ashanti Pioneer*, the opposition groups, including Joe Appiah, Victor Owusu, Paa Willie, K.A. Gbedemah, all formerly prominent colleagues of Nkrumah, went on to emphasise to the nation the disaster to which it was heading. *The Pioneer* was ultimately acquired by the State. Many of the Opposition leaders, including Dr K.A. Busiah, K.A. Gbedemah, the Finance Minister for many years, eventually fled the country, or were imprisoned. An air of fear and repression permeated the whole country, especially from 1st August 1962, when an unsuccessful assassination attempt was made on Nkrumah while he was touring the north of the country.

All political opposition and dissent was violently suppressed by the Special Branch, headed by Mr J.W.K. Harlley. Unofficial censorship and telephone-tapping were secretly introduced and so were exit permits, without which nobody could leave the country. The political arrests continued until, by the time the régime fell, over four thousand persons were in detention without any trial whatsoever. Ironically, a number of those detained included some of the most stalwart defenders and supporters of the régime, among them the head of the Police Force at the time, Mr E.R.T. Madjitey. Following the attempt on Nkrumah's life in 1962, the Police Force had been reorganised, and a few of the top officers sent to the very prisons in which they had been incarcerating others. Nkrumah's right-hand man, Tawiah Adamafio, the Secretary-General of the Party, and Dr Ako Adjei, former Foreign Minister, were all arrested for allegedly being implicated in the plot to kill Nkrumah. Tried, they were acquitted in December 1963 by the Supreme Court, headed by the Chief Justice. Shocked by the Court's ruling, Nkrumah dismissed the Chief Justice and the other judges, and ordered a re-trial, which led to the conviction of the accused. They were sentenced to death!

Doubtful about the loyalty of the Army, Nkrumah created an elite Presidential Guard, which was better equipped and far better provided for, than the normal, regular Army. This Guard was solely responsible for Nkrumah's protection. While the rest of the Army were feeling the economic squeeze, occasioned by the shortage of foreign exchange, the Presidential Guard was in a far more comfortable position. Naturally this state of affairs led to much hostility between the Guard and the rest of the Army. Despite Nkrumah's own often repeated statements that the Army should keep out of politics, he began to interfere in military matters and promotions, playing the two most senior African officers, J.A. Ankrah and S.Otu, against each other, to prevent them getting together to plot a coup. Eventually, both of them were suddenly retired.

Thus by the end of 1965 the country was in a highly nervous, tense state. There were food shortages, tremendous unemployment, the Army was grumbling privately, many people had at least a friend or a relative in prison, the country's currency was heavily devalued and external credit for imports from the West had dried up. Efforts by the régime to replace some of the essential food items such as sugar, sardines, corned beef from the East, were unsuccessful. For the vast majority of the people preferred what they were used to for decades – Western imports. And these were no longer available.

Indeed in November 1965, Ghana had broken diplomatic relations with Britain over the issue of U.D.I. in Rhodesia (Zimbabwe). Even some of the surrounding African countries were beginning to consider Nkrumah, rightly or wrongly, as a destabilising influence in their countries for his alleged interference in their internal affairs. The anti-colonialist, anti-imperialist, pro-marxist public statements and rhetoric continued unabated. However, the fact that, due to the desperate economic conditions of the country, top level delegations had to be despatched to the Western countries to plead for aid and credits as a matter of urgency, made these statements sound hollow, idle and futile. Needless to say, all these delegations returned home with empty hands, after being politely received in the appropriate Western capitals.

By January 1966, the economy was in a desperate state, and Nkrumah faced difficulties on all fronts. He had trouble with some of his African neighbours. He had trouble with his main suppliers and creditors. He had trouble internally over the high cost of living, unemployment, food shortages, the great numbers of people in prison, the constant attacks of the muffled Opposition. The country's foreign reserves were completely depleted, with a huge foreign debt outstanding.

Chapter 3 – The First Coup

24 February 1966

Although the Revolution of June 1979 can be properly said to have had its roots in the coup of January 1972, the second coup in Ghana, it is appropriate here to review the causes and results of the first coup (1966) which ultimately led to the 1972 coup. In the highly charged atmosphere existing in the country at the beginning of 1966, a major event took place in West Africa which was to have direct effects on Ghana. In January 1966, after a series of political disturbances in Nigeria, the first military *coup détat* took place in that country, led by a group of young Sandhurst-trained Nigerian Army Officers. This was the first coup in West Africa, and was to have catastrophic consequences on Ghana. The countries are next door neighbours and former British colonies, with fairly similar colonial backgrounds and heritage. Moreover, for many years there have been direct links between Ghana and Nigeria – the educational, judicial, political and economic systems are similar in both countries.

The coup in Nigeria shook not only that country, but also the surrounding countries, especially Ghana. For many of the reasons which the officers gave for the coup seemed to apply and fit as much to the picture then existing in Ghana. Nkrumah himself went on radio and television on a nation-wide broadcast to comment on the Nigerian situation, stating that the late Prime Minister, Sir Tafewa Balewa, had been overtaken by colonialist, imperialist forces, which he had never understood! After the Nigerian event, and Nkrumah's speech, security was tightened in Ghana, and after completely satisfying himself that everything was in order and the country was in very safe and trustworthy hands, President Nkrumah left Accra on a peace mission to Hanoi at the height of the Vietnam War. It was 22nd February 1966. As always, the chief security, military and police officers, ministers, top party officials, local chiefs and dignitaries, diplomats and a vast, excited crowd were at the airport to see him off. The enthusiastic crowd, drumming, dancing and signing Nkrumah's praises and his invincibility, were all there. Profuse vows to die for the President and the party were publicly repeated, as previously. There was all the evidence that what had happened in Nigeria could simply not happen in Ghana.

Nkrumah and his entourage, practically the whole Cabinet, including the High Commissioner-designate for London and other prominent party officials, left Accra airport *en route* for Hanoi, via Cairo and Peking. At Cairo airport, President Nasser was quoted as having asked Nkrumah whether everything was all right in Ghana, and he replied that indeed things were normal and peaceful, and there were no problems. Nasser had good cause to worry for his good friend, for among other things, Nkrumah's wife was Egyptian, and the marriage had gone a long way in cementing Ghana-Arab relationships.

From Cairo, the Presidential plane headed towards Peking. Alas, while he was in the plane heading for Peking, the Chinese had received the message that the "impossible" had happened in Ghana.

For long before Nkrumah's departure, a group of Army officers led by Colonel E.K. Kotoka, Major A.A. Afrifa, Major V. Coker-Appiah, and Brigadier A.C. Ocran had, after much anguish and misgivings, come to the conclusion that the only way to redeem the country and save it from complete disaster was to remove Nkrumah and bring the C.P.P. régime to an end.

Previous attempts by the first two officers had failed through leaks or last minute changes of mind. This time, in co-operation with the Police Chief, Mr J.W.K. Harlley, and his deputy Mr A.C. Deku, the Army officers were determined to strike to end Nkrumah's rule, which by that time had become dictatorial, corrupt, tyrannical and unbearable for many people.

In the early hours of 24th February 1966, the Police effected the swift and complete arrest of all the Cabinet Ministers, top party functionaries and officials, all regional commissioners, district commissioners and party officials. By the time the Police acted, a battalion of troops from Ashanti and the north, on the pretext of conducting training manoeuvres in preparation for their despatch to Rhodesia, had reached Accra, having covered a distance of over 180 miles through difficult territory during the previous day. They were led by Colonel Kotoka and Major Afrifa. Joining their comrades in Accra, under the command of Brigadier Ocran, they quietly set into motion the whole military operation. Senior officers who were not in favour of the coup were locked up, and those of them resisting arrest, including the Army Commander, General Barwah, were shot dead. The airport was sealed off. The land borders were all closed to prevent any escape to the surrounding countries. The telephone system in Accra was cut off. The Army Headquarters at Burma Camp was rapidly captured with no resistance whatsoever. Swiftly the Broadcasting House, the Castle – which was the headquarters of the Government – the General Post Office, and the Cable and Wireless Building were all taken over without resistance.

By 5.30am on 24th February 1966 a stunned nation heard the voice of Major Afrifa announce that Nkrumah's régime had been toppled in an Army coup, and were introduced to Colonel Kotoka, the architect of the coup. After giving the reasons for the coup, enumerating the charges of corruption, bribery, nepotism, economic mismanagement, moral depravity, oppression, tyranny, dictatorship etc., against the defunct régime, all ministers and party officials and certain specified persons not yet arrested were asked to report to the nearest police stations to be imprisoned for their own protection – or face the consequences.

Although the commanding heights of the Government had quickly collapsed like a pack of cards, the citadel of Nkrumah's rule, Flagstaff House, in Accra, which was both his office and residence was still defying defeat. There, the Presidential Guard, under the command of Colonel Zelarungu, put up a spirited defence from the early hours of 24 February until about 12.30 in the afternoon. By that time, outgunned, outmanoeuvred and hopelessly outnumbered, the Guard, under its commander, surrendered to the liberation forces. About twenty men were killed and many were injured. So ended the fiften-year rule of Nkrumah. Looking back, it is amazing how easily the whole régime collapsed, like a pack of cards.

Swiftly all prominent supporters and intellectual defenders of the régime were arrested and sent to prison. They included the former British Labour MP Mr Geoffrey Bing, who had become advisor to Nkrumah, after serving first as constitutional advisor, and later as Attorney-General. To make room for the new prison arrivals, all the political prisoners incarcerated by the previous régime, numbering about 4000 people, were released in batches. They included some old and infirm men and women, some of whom died shortly afterwards. They included people from all walks of life – farmers, politicians, academics, students, market women, journalists, lawyers etc. They included three of Nkrumah's most powerful supporters, Tawiah Adamafio, Dr Ako Adjei, Cofie Crabbe and others who had been condemned to death by the second trial for allegedly being implicated in the assassination attempt on Nkrumah in August 1962.

While the arrests of the former ministers and party stalwarts were gong on, the masses, who had previously poured on the streets to demonstrate *for* Nkrumah and pledge their unflinching loyalty to the régime, poured out again on the streets to demonstrate, this time *against* Nkrumah and the régime, and to pledge their support for the new régime. The so-called "imperialist stooges", "C.I.A. agents", "Colonialist boot-lickers", had suddenly become national heroes overnight and the "strong revolutionaries" of yesterday were either in prison or wisely hiding. A few lucky ones were able to flee the country before it was impossible to do so.

Considering the relative ease with which an apparently invincible and powerful régime was destroyed, one is bound to conclude that by the time of the régime's demise, its most prominent supporters had lost heart. Apart from the Presidential Guard, there was no effective, organised challenge from any quarter. It appeared that all the supporters of the régime threw in their lot with the new régime once the initial military moves against it had been made. Certainly there were no public demonstrations for the ousted régime. What happened was the very opposite of what one might have expected or guessed a few days before 24th February 1966. The emotional and psychological impact of the coup on many people, especially certain leading supporters of the régime, was incalculable. The incidence of nervous breakdown, and the high mortality rate among these people, could well be related to the unexpected events of 24th February 1966. Nobody in his wildest dreams, thought that the Nkrumah régime could ever be removed.

Nkrumah, hearing of the collapse of his régime from the Chinese could not at first believe it. Nor did he believe in the BBC news report. However, after checking with the Ghana Embassies in Paris and London, the truth finally sank in – that the impossible had happened. He was in a state of shock, but still had recovered sufficiently to attend a state dinner which was being given that night in his honour as the "President of Ghana". According to a Minister in his entourage in Peking, after threatening to bomb the Akosombo Dam, and other industrial installations, Nkrumah recovered himself, and took a more realistic and pragmatic approach to his problem. He asked his Foreign Minister, Alex Quaison-Sackey, to go to the O.A.U. Conference, then currently taking place in Addis Ababa, Ethiopia, and state Ghana's case – that his régime was the legitimate and constitutional government of the country. He asked his London High Commissioner – designate to go to London in order to establish the legitimacy of his régime. Arrangements were made for the hordes of top civil servants, security men, and aides, accompanying him, to return to Accra via London. He himself decided to fly from Peking to Moscow to argue his case for help and assistance. He took with him only a handful of personal aides, security men and followers.

Meanwhile, his Foreign Minister, London High Commissioner and others, left for London. In Frankfurt, the Foreign Minister decided to fly straight to Accra instead of Addis Ababa. Arriving at Accra airport he made his famous statement about how wonderful it was to breathe a whiff of fresh air of freedom. He pledged his allegiance to the military régime, was given the customary military double-up and sent to prison to join his colleagues. Luckily for him, a few months later he was released and allowed to go to Britain, where he went to study law and qualified as a barrister.

The London High Commissioner – designate, with his family already in the official residence, pending the presentation of his credentials to the Court of St James, left for Accra, after a brief sojourn in London. A doctor by profession, he was briefly interred and then employed in the Government health service. The former London High Commissioner, then Trade Minister, decided to stay in London, where he successfully fought a long legal battle for his extradition to Accra on criminal charges, involving misappropriation of state funds.

Nkrumah himself, after a few days' stay in Moscow, flew on to Conakry, the capital of Guinea. There he was given an emotional and enthusiastic presidential welcome. He was given the title "Co-President of Guinea". In Guinea, Nkrumah initially spent some time broadcasting to Ghana. These broadcasts soon ceased and he spent the rest of his life writing on Ghana and African affairs, and on neo-colonialism, improving his French and receiving visits from some of his colleagues who were outside Ghana. Subsequently, he developed cancer of the skin, was sent to Rumania for treatment, where he eventually died in April 1972. A violent public controversy arose over the disposition of his body, but eventually it was brought to Ghana and given a full state burial by the second military régime.

Meanwhile, following the collapse of the Nkrumah administration, the first military régime in Ghana had constituted itself into a Government, under the name of the National Liberation Council (N.L.C.).

It quickly started to liberate the country not only politically but also economically. After the release of the thousands of political detainees and prisoners of the Nkrumah period, commissions of enquiry were set up to investigate prison conditions and the allegations of brutality and inhuman treatment which were alleged to have been meted out in these prisons. Investigations were also conducted into the causes of the death of Dr J.B. Danquah, Obetsebi Lamptey, and others who had died or disappeared in detention. The Government voted a rehabilitation fund for the prison victims of the Nkrumah régime.

The Civil Service was reorganised and in the process a number of persons lost their jobs.

The retrogressive and oppressive laws which had been enacted in the Nkrumah period were quickly repealed. Press freedom was restored, and new editors were appointed for the State papers (*Ghanaian Times, Daily Graphic,* and *Pioneer*) as the previous editors had gone to prison following the coup. Similar reorganisation was undertaken in the radio and television services. The more outspoken, rabidly anti-western radio commentators lost their jobs, to be replaced by more moderate and pragmatic writers and commentators.

To deal with the endemic bribery and corruption in the country, a number of Commissions of Enquiry headed by eminent High Court judges were appointed. They were charged with the duty of investigating the sources and means of acquisition of the assets of the ministers, top party officials – and their wives – of the previous régime. A decree was issued freezing all the assets and bank accounts of these persons. Their assets and funds thus became state property, and could not be sold or disposed of, or transferred without Government approval. Their wives, although not arrested, could only withdraw certain limited amounts from their husbands' accounts or their own, and that only after appropriate sanction by the Attorney-General's Office.

Their husbands, while in prison, were given long questionnaires to complete. The questionnaires covered such matters as birth, education, marriage, employment, salaries and expenditure, year by year, right to the day of the coup. Overseas trips, fares, hotel expenses, properties (abroad and local), jewellery, household furniture, cars, savings, investments (both local and abroad) all had to be accounted for in the appropriate columns. A heavy prison sentence was the price to be paid for any attempt to hide certain facts and figures, if one was unfortunate enough to be caught. The specified persons in prison, and their wives, were then called one by one, to face the Commissions of

Enquiry. Access to lawyers was allowed for those who could afford them. These Commissions of Enquiry gave the persons concerned the opportunity to defend their assets and those of their families. The whole proceedings were held with the public, the press, radio and television present. Apart from defending their assets, many of the former ministers and party officials took the grand opportunity to condemn violently and punish their Government, especially their leader, President Nkrumah. One by one, many shifted the blame for every wrong doing on Nkrumah, and stated that they knew nothing about the bribery and corruption then rampant. Ironically, it was chiefly the "socialist boys" (who had not enriched themselves during the period) who faithfully and consistently stood up for the régime!

In 1967-68, the reports of these Commissions and the accompanying White Papers prepared on them by the Attorney-General's Office were published. They fully established what had been public knowledge all the while – that many of these persons were corrupt, and had acquired assets and funds somehow which could not be properly accounted for on their known salaries or other sources of income. All the assets, e.g. homes, buildings and funds which, in the opinion of the Commissions, had not been properly and satisfactorily explained, as to their sources, were recommended to be confiscated by the state. Many lost homes, cars and substantial sums of money. In some cases criminal prosecutions followed with their conviction, and imprisonment as criminals.

To exorcise the marxist strain from the body politic, a Commission was set up to which all persons who had been members of certain specified organisations had to appear for clearance, before they could hold public office in future.

Although in full control, the first military régime did not make the mistake of becoming too involved in the detailed running of the country. They concentrated on the reorganisation of the

Armed Forces and the Police Service. The Presidential Guard was dissolved and re-absorbed into the regular army, after a few essential discharges had been effected. The image of the Army was refurbished, and those considered as irresponsible elements were retired. Similarly, the Police Force Special Branch, after suffering a number of dismissals, was re-absorbed into the regular Police Force.

A few of the members of the N.L.C. were allocated civilian positions as ministers, under the name of "Commissioners". The regions were headed administratively by senior military officers, usually Colonels. A handful of senior officers were appointed Ambassadors. But, by and large, the civilian administration of the country remained intact. Prominent civilians, mostly academics and experienced industrialists, were appointed as Commissioners to replace the imprisoned Nkrumah Ministers. Otherwise, the military régime of the N.L.C., under the chairmanship of General J.A. Ankrah, did not interfere very significantly with the administration of the country. They kept scrupulously to their declared aims of the coup, namely, to get rid of the Nkrumah dictatorship, rid the country of bribery, corruption and immorality, restore democracy and stop the drift to economic bankruptcy facing the country.

Towards the restoration of democracy, a number of committees were set up to prepare for the immediate return to civilian democratic rule. A political committee was established to guide and advise the military government on the administration of the country. A committee was set up to go into Chieftaincy affairs, and review the plethora of disputes around chiefs, many of whom had been foistered on their people during the Nkrumah régime. Committees were set up to go into every aspect of the fifteen years of the Nkrumah. The Universities, the Civil Service, the State Corporations were all subjected to vigorous scrutiny with military precision.

Repeatedly, the N.L.C. told the public that it was not interested in hanging on to public office indefinately, and they were anxious to return to the barracks at the earliest possible time. They appeared genuinely determined to do the improbable – the peaceful surrender of public office by a military government to a civilian government duly-elected by the people.

This commitment to democratic government on the Western model was freely and frequently repeated in public. It was hard to believe whether it would all come out as being promised. The public were sceptical, for it sounded too good to be true. Were these people who were enjoying plush, civilian jobs for the first time in their lives – jobs which carried with them a lot of perks, such as large chauffeur-driven Mercedes cars, tremendous political patronage, the attentions of beautiful women, free drinks, etc, going to give them all up and go back to their former strict military lives? The public's view was to wait and see!

A constitutional Commission was set up under Akuffo-Addo, a former Supreme Court Judge, who had been dismissed by Nkrumah in 1963 over the trial and acquittal of his political associates, who had been charged with being involved in the assassination attempt on Nkrumah. The Commission travelled all over the country; holding public sessions in the various regional centres, accepting oral and written memoranda on the country's future constitution to replace the past one of the Nkrumah régime. Many prominent citizens and organisations including the Churches, Students, the Bar Association, freely presented their views to the Commission. These were all collated, studied and analysed, and out of them finally came the Commission's Draft Constituion for Ghana, which was published in 1968.

All over the country people were exercising their freedom and enjoying in a way which they had never done before, except for the heydays of independence, in 1958-59. The press, radio and television, although state-owned and controlled, were free for all practical purposes. Divergent views could now be freely expressed, without fear of arbitrary arrest. The air of freedom was indeed "fresh and wonderful", to quote Alex Quaison-Sackey.

For a military régime, the N.L.C. kept an extremely low profile, and many Ghanaians, accustomed to the days of "strong government" of the Nkrumah era, could really not believe their eyes and ears that they were now so free. The irony was that this was happening under a military government.

Hundreds of exiles, prominent and not-so-prominent, who had run away from the country at the heydays of the Nkrumah régime began to return home to receive tumultous, public welcome. They included such men as K.A. Gbedemah (Finance Minister under Nkrumah for many years), Dr K.A. Busia (Opposition Leader for many years), Prof. de Graft Johnson, Oheneba Kow Richardson, Yaw Manu, etc. Making their triumphal return, they felt their cause had been vindicated by the coup of 24 February 1966, and the subsequent events. As these people rejoiced, the former defenders of the defunct régime tried to keep as low a public profile as possible behaving, in many cases, as if they did not exist.

To repair the damage which had been done to the image of the country by Nkrumah's frequent anti-western public statements, a high-powered Government delegation was sent to these countries to inform them officially of the new wind of change blowing through Ghana. Such measures were vital in the neighbouring African states which, before Nkrumah's fall, had not looked on happily to what they considered to be the undue and unnecessary interference in their internal affairs by Nkrumah. The missions to these countries were given a very friendly welcome, and suddenly Ghana had friends again, both near and far.

There was a definite and unashamed effort to re-establish Ghana's traditional links and contacts in all fields, with the West. The previous drift towards re-writing the country's history, by reversing its traditional pro-Western trends in trade, education, politics, and other spheres of human endeavour, were positively and clearly halted.

Lastly, it would be worth mentioning here that towards the end of his régime, Nkrumah realised belatedly that his unsocialist "socialist colleagues" were doing his political party's name and image a great deal of harm in the public eye. He resorted to the strategy of attacking their greed and corruption through the press, which were controlled by his ardent followers. I was in 1964 told the story of how two of Nkrumah's ministers after recieving a blistering attack in one of the state papers for their alleged avarice, bribery and corruption, had gone to the President to complain bitterly over their public humiliation and disgrace. Pacified by the President, they went on their way to confront the editor concerned for the attacks, and to demand an apology. While they were with the editor, his telephone rang. Who was on the phone at the other end but Nkrumah himself, congratulating the editor on the blistering attack of the previous day's editorial and asking for a repeat? Thus, as the editor faced the two ministers before him, he was seething with a mixture of anger and amusement, could hardly repress his true feelings, and was bursting to say "Gentlemen, you are wasting my time and yours. Please be gone!"

As a final effort to remove from public life his old partners of many years whose public activities and public image were a positive liability, Nkrumah packed the last Parliament, with many hand-picked, bright new faces with unblemished public reputations. They were not elected, but nominated by the party's Central Committee and foistered on the masses. The "General Elections" of 1965, under the one-party state constitution were the last to be held in Ghana. By the time the next elections were held in the country, conditions, both political and economic, had changed most drastically.

Chapter 4 –

The pendulum swings from left to centre

On the economic front, the situation at the time the National Liberation Council took over was that there were acute food shortages, of both local and imported food, the cost of living was unbearably high, unemployment was massive (about 50 per cent) and the position of the country's balance of payment was very serious. Indeed, the Bureau of Statistics and the Bank of Ghana had been issuing periodic warnings in their annual reports about the looming danger and economic catastrophe before the coup. By February 1966, Ghana owed the outside world at least 1,000 million US dollars. Most of these debts were short and medium-term credits, owed to both the West and East, but chiefly to the former. And among the Western creditors, Britain was owed the most.

The situation was desperate and needed immediate and forthright solution. Following the political liberation of the people in February 1966, they looked fervently to their economic liberation too. They expected the empty shelves in the shops to be filled, the food queues to disappear, more drugs and medicines to arrive for the hospitals and clinics, the chronic shortages of such essential items as sardines, corned beef, sugar, toothpaste and toilet rolls to end. In short, they expected as complete a break as possible with the economic past.

Having brought to Ghanaians the political kingdom of liberty and personal freedom, the first military régime – the N.L.C. – set about bringing also the economic kingdom of sufficient food, adequate supply of medicines, drugs, spare parts for vehicles, building materials and other essential commodities which had for long disappeared from the Ghanaian scene.

The Government first of all turned its attention to a drastic pruning of public expenditure, where there was a great deal of waste. Commissions of enquiry were set up into the activities of all the major State and semi-State Corporations, in order to assess their usefulness to the national economy, their efficiency, and their cost-benefit contribution to the nation. The over-manning, inefficiency, bribery, corruption and nepotism which were unearthed in these corporations by the commissions were beyond belief. Admittedly, long before these commissions were set up, long before the coup itself, it was well known to many intelligent citizens and residents in the country that there was immense corruption, nepotism and inefficiency rampant in all these corporations. But the full extent could only be revealed by the reports of these Commissions. Following their recom-mendations, and their accompanying White Papers, the Govern-ment went ahead, full steam, to rationalise the economy and bring discipline into it, acting on the advice contained in these documents, and also on that of local private businessmen and women.

Some of the corporations were drastically pruned in scope and activities, while some such as the Workers' Brigade were completely abolished. The Workers' Brigade was a civilian, para-military organisation which had been set up in the Nkrumah régime as a work force to undertake such activities as con-struction, farming and road building. However, towards the later stages of the régime, it had become more readily available as a source of human material for "spontaneous demonstrations" against not only "imperialists", "colonialists", etc, but also prominent local businessmen and other political opponents of the régime.

Those corporations which escaped the axe were vigorously reorganised, shedding in the process some of their former senior personnel and staff.

Investigations into Government contracts and agreements, chiefly with foreign firms and a few local business entrepreneurs revealed the same story of wanton corruption, inflated pricing, and a general disregard for the best interests of the country. The reports of the various commissions again show that certain foreign businessmen and their Ghanaian ministerial accomplices, had done untold damage and harm to the country's economy. Although the economic pendulum of the nation, following Nkrumah's fall, swung from left towards the right, it would be wrong to give the impression that there was a violent swing to the extreme right. This was not the case. After fifteen years of the Nkrumah régime, such a deep foundation of socialist theory and practice in the country, and among the people, had been laid that it would have been politically suicidal, even for a military government, to have tried to reverse too drastically the trend of economic affairs. The people had come to take for granted the traditional benefits of the welfare state, such as free schooling, free medical care (where available), heavily subsidised housing, subsidised transport, subsidised food, water etc., that there would have been an outright revolt if the military government had set out, openly and positively, to reduce or remove these social benefits.

The N.L.C. all along repeated its commitment to making the nation's economy more efficient and less corrupt and returning the country to civilian rule as early as possible. As such, it did not consider it as its duty to interfere unduly with the economic set-up of the nation. However, the net result of the new politics of the country was to bring it in confirmity with the country's traditional foreign policy of non-alignment. The anti-Western, pro-East radio and television broadcasts and comments were terminated, and a determined effort was made by the N.L.C. to woo the friendship and investment of the West. After declaring, on the day of the coup (February 24 1966) that the new Ghana Government would fulfil all Ghana's debts and external financial obligations which the new Government had inherited, it quickly (in March 1966) sent powerful economic delegations to the major Western capitals to repair the damage of the past and seek fresh financial help and aid for Ghana. These delegations were warmly welcomed wherever they went. Furthermore, the Western countries quickly responded to Ghana's pleas. Fresh aid credits were granted, and help in various forms began to pour in. Prominent among the aid-donors were Britain, West Germany, and the USA. Soon the shops began to be full of the essential food items and commodities which they had not seen for quite a few years. Although these items were coming into the country on credit, the fact still remains that from the point of view of the man in the street, these goods and food items were now available. How they were obtained, from whence they came, or under what terms, was irrelevant at that time.

To help the export of Ghana's produce, the local currency – the cedi – was devalued in 1967, and many of the choking restrictions on trade were removed or relaxed. There was a general policy to liberalise the economy in order to encourage hard work and private initiative, and to enhance the work ethic. The fact that the country had been living extravagantly on borrowed money, borrowed food and borrowed time was openly and vividly brought to the realisation of the public by radio and television. What had previously been hidden from the public – the huge internal and foreign debt of the Government – was now spelt out in no uncertain terms. The people were told plainly that the days of free health services, state subsidised housing, employment, transport, education had to end, for the country could no longer afford them. Although these welfare state measures had been introduced in the late 1950s when Ghana had a healthy balance of payment, later, especially in the mid-1960s, when the price and production of cocoa were falling, it was no longer economically possible to maintain the previous levels of public expenditure. Alas, it was *politically* impossible to turn back to the past. The people had come to enjoy and expect these welfare state programmes as a matter of course. The Nkrumah régime, therefore, continued to borrow and borrow, till it could borrow no more!

For the first military régime, spelling out the truth to the people was no problem. Firstly, they were committed to reversing the past economic trends. Secondly, they were not electorally obliged to the people for support, as the previous Government was. As part of the process of instilling discipline into the national economy, the whole programme of scholarship awards for overseas study, which was costing the country millions of pounds, was subjected to thorough scrutiny by Colonel George Bernasko, who was then head of the education section of the Armed Forces. As a result of his personal investigations and interviews, hundreds of scholarships which were being utilised by Ghana students abroad, who were either not studying or had long ceased to study, and had become "professional students", were immediately withdrawn. Subsequently, fresh scholarships and awards were granted to more deserving students.

It can be stated, without fear of contradiction, that the N.L.C. by the time it left the political scene in October 1969 had brought immense improvement to the state of the Ghana economy. It would be idle to suggest that it was able to eradicate bribery and corruption completely. How could it do so in three years when the disease had taken decades to take root? However, it brought corruption, inefficiency and nepotism to low, tolerable levels in the country. And that was indeed an immense achievement!

What the N.L.C. did to the economy was to revitalise and rejuvenate it by borrowing more, and requesting and receiving more aid and help from the West. With the economy revitalised, the military Government was able to pay more of the nation's debts. Consequently, by the time the military were leaving the scene in order to return to the barracks, the estimated external debts of the nation stood at about 1,000 million US dollars – the same amount as when they took over from the Nkrumah régime. However, through their negotiations for the repayment of the debts Ghana owed to the outside world, especially the West, the N.L.C. injected more confidence into the Ghana economy, and thus set it off on the road to recovery.

In order to save foreign exchange, which could be better employed towards providing more water supply and medical facilities for the people, a thorough review of the foreign service was undertaken. As a result, about twenty embassies were closed down, leaving about forty. In the heyday of Ghana's Independence, when other African countries looked up to Ghana as the first African state to become independent in modern times, Nkrumah's policy of opening embassies almost world-wide could be justified. In the mid-1960s when more African countries had, with Ghana's help, directly and indirectly, become free and independent, the need to maintain embassies throughout Africa and in all the major capitals of the world could no longer be justified. Moreover, the country's own economic situation made such a policy difficult to maintain. The N.L.C.s decision to close some of the embassies and to reduce the staff of the rest was accepted by most people as being in the best interests of the country.

This action of the N.L.C. in closing a number of embassies after the coup has been criticised for having led to a diminution in the international image of Ghana, and to a reduction of her influence in Africa. The fact still remains that by the time these embassies were closed down, the country was bankrupt, and this was well known to both the friends and adversaries of Ghana. As such, her effort to project a strong international image from a weak economic position was really futile. Indeed, it effectively made Ghana the butt of rather cruel diplomatic jokes – the poor relation who had seen better and long forgotten days, trying hard to relive the good old days! Thus the N.L.C. decision, as with many things which they did, was one more attempt to discipline the country and literally force it to live within its means.

What then can be said to be the main achievements of Ghana's first military régime by the time of its departure from the political scene? Firstly, they firmly and solidly returned Ghana into its traditional, pro-British, pro-Western, pro-capitalist orbit. This was to lead to a revitalisation of the economy, and the resumption of aid and financial assistance from various Western nations. There lies a lesson for all post-revolutionary Governments in Ghana – that while any Ghana Government is entitled to be as anti-West and as anti-capitalist as it wishes, it would have to face the inescapable logic of such a situation, namely the drastic reduction in Western aid and assistance which such a policy brings in its wake. The lesson may be put in another way – if you wish to be violently and publicly anti-capitalist, then you should not in the same breath ask for or expect economic aid and assistance from the capitalist West. Secondly, the N.L.C. were able to fulfil the basic needs of the people by quickly providing sufficient food – both local and foreign – medicines and drugs, and spare parts. Thirdly, there was a tremendous expansion in the provision of good drinking water to a greater proportion of the population than had ever been provided by any previous régime. Fourthly, the N.L.C. helped to reduce the level of corruption and hypocrisy in public life, by releasing future political leaders from the constraints of having to preach "socialism" in public, and live and practice "capitalism" in private lives. The economic policies of the N.L.C. were further extended by the Government that followed them in October 1969.

Chapter 5 – Restoration of Democracy

The main reason which had been given by the first military régime for the coup of 1966 was the need to restore democracy in Ghana and to end the one-man rule of Nkrumah. This objective was often emphasised by the members of the N.L.C. in their public statements. However, many people took these statements with a large dose of disbelief for it sounded too good to be true – a military Government voluntarily working itself out of office to the benefit of a civilian Government! Besides, so many people were so mindful of the last cruel and callous days of the defunct régime that if the N.L.C. had stated that they were going to stay in power for the next ten or fifteen years – as long as the régime they had just overthrown – there would have been mass public acclamation for this decision. Indeed, in many speeches and public statements by some chiefs, as traditional rulers and representatives of their people, the request for the military Government to stay in power for a fairly long time was frequently made. To some extent this behaviour was not surprising.

With the C.P.P. leaders and supporters effectively out of the political scene, either in jail or quietly keeping a low profile in public, and with the former political opponents of Nkrumah just returning from exile or beginning to regroup, the pleas for a quick return to democratic, civilian rule could effectively come only from the anti-Nkrumah groups. Many people felt happier and better off under the military régime than they had been under the civilian one. The obvious exception being the leaders and prominent supporters of the overthrown régime and their families, friends and relatives.

The clamour for the early return to civilian rule thus came chiefly from the anti-Nkrumah groups. All the others, including some prominent chiefs, trade-unionists, academics and journalists, because of their over-enthusiastic endorsement of the overthrown régime, had done so much damage and harm to their own names and credibility that any talk by them about "democracy", "civilian rule", "human rights", would have brought on their heads the wrath of the public. And they were too clever for that.

Spear-heading the appeal for an early return to civilian rule was Prof. K.A. Busia, an eminent sociologist and author, who had for many years been a strong critic of Dr Nkrumah's dictatorial policies and Marxist economic policies and ideas. After leading the Opposition in Parliament, he had found it prudent at the height of the excesses of the Nkrumah régime to flee the country in 1959 for refuge in Britain. From there he toured Europe, U.S.A. and Africa informing people about the excesses of the Nkrumah régime and the gloomy future that lay ahead of the nation if nothing was done by the outside world, especially by the West, to bring the régime down. Although he was sympathetically received wherever he went, there is no evidence to suggest that he ever received the amount of moral and financial support which could have effectively been utilised to topple the Nkrumah régime, which, to all intents and purposes, was impregnable and invincible. Using his modest home in Oxford, as his base, he lectured, wrote, travelled, from 1960-1966, calling for democracy in Africa in general, and in Ghana, particularly.

Returning to Ghana in February 1966, a few days after the coup, he was given a nation-wide, tumultous welcome. He had been proved right! As Dr Danquah had died in Nkrumah's prison in 1965, Dr Busia was the national successor to replace him. Logic and commonsense demanded it, and so he did. Dr Busia was appointed to a few important national committees, and eventually he was appointed Chairman of the Centre for Civic Education. This was an organisation which had been set up by the N.L.C., on the lines of adult-education programmes, to teach the masses – from the towns, right to the most humble hamlets – about their democratic rights, human rights, government abuse of power, voting, elections, etc. As the previous government had laid so much emphasis nationwide on the citizen's obligations to the State, and no emphasis on the aformentioned subjects, it was right that new and heavy emphasis should be placed on the citizen's rights and the State's legal and moral obligation to the citizen. The evils of dictatorship, one-man rule, communism, repression, arbitrary rule, which had long been swept under the carpet, had to be fully exposed to the fresh sweep and action of a fresh political and constitutional vacuum-cleaner.

This was the job which the Centre for Civic Education set out to do in 1968. Naturally, the leader of this organisation by virtue of his postion, had to travel the length and breadth of the nation, to do his job properly. He was in an excellent position to expose himself politically to the nation. The reception which he received everywhere positively indicated that the people expected him to be their new leader and ruler. Considering that there was a ban on politics and political activities since the day of the coup in February 1966, Dr Busia's position as Chairman of the Centre for Civic Education gave him and his political colleagues a great deal of advantage when full political activities were eventually allowed by the military régime in April 1969. It is conceivable that even without the huge advantage which his new public position gave him, Busia, as a direct result of the coup itself, would have become the natural post-coup leader without much trouble. His life had become the story of the prophet being

67

honoured among his own people and in his own country.

While the Centre for Civic Education continued its work, the members of the N.L.C. also made their contribution to the restoration of democracy in the country. Apart from governing the nation, they made frequent, public speeches and statements condemning the Nkrumah régime, socialism, dictatorship, tyranny, and other evil manifestations of the overthrown régime. Also because of the vast credibility gap between the public calls for *socialism* by the leading members of the Nkrumah régime, and the private lives and activities of some of these same people, the term "socialism" had become most-abhorred by the public. It had become synonymous with deceit, bribery, corruption and a free-for-all, *laissez-faire* economic policy.

The extent of the damage which had been done to socialism, by the "socialism" of the Nkrumah period, can be gauged by the fact that right up to June 1979, when the political inheritors of the Nkrumah party re-grouped and re-launched themselves as the People's National Party, they found it wise and prudent not to mention the word socialism, not even once, in their political manifesto. Perhaps they had learnt from the bitter mistakes of the past.

The return to democratic civilian rule was given a major boost, with the publication of the report of the Constitutional Commission chaired by Justice Akuffo-Addo. The Commission submitted a draft constitution for Ghana, which tried, as much as humanly possible to close all the constitutional loopholes of the past which were exploited into dictatorship and tyranny. The independence of the judiciary was guaranteed. Freedom of the press and human rights were guaranteed. Freedom of movement, speech, religion, assembly were all guaranteed. Already well-versed in the British Constitution, the Commission consulted the West German and American Constitutions, taking oral and documentary evidence where necessary. Ultimately, the draft which the Commission produced was accepted by the military Government. Following that, 150 representatives of various shades of opinion and vocations were elected from the Universities, Bar Association, Medical Association, the Chiefs, Junior and Senior Civil Service, the Farmers' Union, the Market Women's Association, the Judiciary, Trade Unionists, Journalists etc. From January to August, 1969 the draft Constitution was vigorously debated by the Constituent Assembly in Accra. As a member myself of this historic Assembly, I remember vividly the constant refrain in the Assembly and its corridors – *never again should dictatorship and one-man rule thrive in Ghana.* That was one major issue that all the men and women who were taking part in the deliberations of the Assembly agreed upon.

Eventually, after long debates, a Constitution was agreed on, which was as good a human document as could be devised. After enshrining all the basic human rights and freedoms, the new Constitution provided for a President – holding nominal powers – with a Prime Minister – the leader of the majority party in Parliament. The Leader of Opposition was officially recognised and subsequently a salary was fixed for him. The Government was to resign on being defeated on a major vote of confidence in Parliament. The President was elected by Parliament (but not from it) from a selection of candidates who put themselves before it for election to the high office of President. The Constitution was very similar to that of Britain, except for the provision for a President instead of a Monarch.

The N.L.C. without interfering in any way with the Constitution accepted it in August 1969, and it was promulgated as the new Constitution of the Second Republic with effect from 1 October 1969. Meanwhile, a new Electoral Commission, under the chairmanship of Justice V.R.A.C. Crabbe – a man renowned for his honesty, public probity, fearlessness and even his religious accomplishment as a devout Yoga devotee – was set up. It quickly started the registration of all Ghanaians of 21 years age and above eligible to vote under the new Constitution.

As the progress towards a return to civilian rule went on, a major political event took place whose significance for the future was to become more evident about twelve years later when the Revolution of June 1979 took place. In April 1967, when the Military Government had been in office for only about fourteen months, there was an attempted coup by a small group of Army officers to dislodge the N.L.C. from office. Based in HO, with the Medium Mortar régiment, about 120 miles from Accra, Lieutenants Arthur, Yeboah and Second Lieutenant Poku, all young men in their twenties, led a small contingent of about 100 men of the Reconnaissance squadron towards Accra. The ostensible reason which the soldiers were given was that there was an attempted coup against the military régime in Accra and that they had been ordered to go to Accra to help quell it. Starting with six armoured cars, one of the leaders of the coup even had the nerve and confidence enough to report his journey to the duty sergeant at the Police-Station in HO, in front of which the column of armoured cars and vehicles was passing. At dawn on 24 April 1967 the sergeant even gave a message to be relayed to his sister who lived at Burma Camp, Accra, the head-quarters of the Ghana Armed Forces!

So far so good. However, it appeared that the gods were not on the side of the coup-makers. First of all, on the way to Accra, one of the armoured cars broke down, another developed engine difficulties, and a third was short of fuel. By the time they were supposed to be in Accra, i.e. about 3 a.m., they were still on the road, bogged down by mechanical problems. Eventually, the broken down vehicles were abandoned and the contingent reached Accra by about 5 a.m. with only three of their vehicles. Surprisingly, they were able to quickly and easily capture the radio station (the chief target in all coups), Burma Camp (the military headquarters), the Castle (the seat of Government) and the Flagstaff House (Nkrumah's former office and residence, then the Army Headquarters). There they killed the chief architect of the 1966 Coup, General Kotoka, and three junior officers. Thus within a couple of hours, the capital was in the hands of the mutineers.

Lieutenant Arthur, their leader then announced on the radio the real reasons for the coup – the unhappiness of the junior officers as they watched their senior officers give rapid promotions to themselves, while the rest of them kept marking time. They were also envious of the new financial and material advantages which had accrued to some of their senior officers since they became associated with the administration of the country following the coup. This was the first sign of any politicisation of the Army and its involvement directly in the administration of the nation, which was bound to, sooner or later, yield a dangerous fall-out on the Army itself. The longer the period of involvement, the greater the danger. For by the very nature of things, due to the very limited nature of the civilian jobs available, it meant that only a few, trusted or favourite officers or friends of the military Government could be found civilian jobs. The jobs were limited in number, and the soldiers did not have the necessary training, aptitude and experience. Thus the few who were selected and given civilian jobs suddenly came to hold great financial and personal advantages over their colleagues who were not so fortunate. This would happen even if they did not receive any emoluments for the extra civilian responsibilities which they had come to assume.

Secondly, a prolonged military involvement in civilian administration tended to corrupt the soldiers. For, as normal human beings, no different from their civilian brothers and sisters, except that temporarily they were armed and in uniform,

71

they were bound to be affected by the indemic bribery and corruption and nepotism prevailing in the civilian system, once they got involved too deeply in it. This was inevitable.

Thirdly, if the military involvement was too long, apart from the two effects mentioned above, it was very likely to lead to command difficulties in the Army itself, as more and more of their best men were seconded to the easier, quieter, money-conscious civilian administration.

These were some of the major problems which were high-lighted by military administration in Ghana, and it took "Arthur's coup" to bring them to the serious attention of the public and the Army itself. Although the coup was quickly suppressed (it lasted only about six hours) it showed how dangerous it is for any Ghana Government to rely exclusively on the Special Branch, Military Intelligence and other security agencies for its continued existence. It could not be easily explained how, with all these agencies in existence, it had been possible, despite telephone-tapping, bugging, censoring of mail etc. for a contingent of armoured cars and men to openly and freely travel 120 miles towards the capital. Following this incident the security forces were thoroughly re-organised but ironically, further coups could still not be stopped.

After the quelling of "Arthur's coup", Arthur and Yeboah were both publicly executed, by firing squad, the first in Ghana's history. Their third accomplice, Second Lieutenant Poku, was sentenced to life imprisonment and sent to Ussher Fort Prison, Accra. Following the coup of January 1972, Poku was released by the second military régime, and has become a successful and prosperous newspaper publisher.

It appears that the first military régime learnt a lesson from the partial success of Arthur's coup. The urgency for an early return to civilian rule was often emphasised in public statements which were made after the abortive coup.

As the march towards civilian rule went on unabated, and preparations towards that event were feverishly taking place, the whole political climate became murky with rumours of friction among the members of the military Government – rumours that some of them were corrupt, rumours that some of them, having tasted the sweets of political power, were not too keen for an early return to civilian rule, despite their public statements to the contrary. There were rumours that some of the officers seconded to civilian jobs had also begun to catch the same civilian disease of bribery, corruption, nepotism and other social evils which their Government had set out to uproot or check. There were rumours of threats by some of the members of the N.L.C. to resign and force into the open certain issues, which should be publicly-aired.

There were also rumours of a major rift between Komla Gbedemah, the veteran Finance Minister under Nkrumah for many years, who had to flee the country in 1964 to avoid arrest, and had been in exile till the coup, and Dr K.A. Busia, the former leader of Opposition, who, in exile had collaborated with Gbedemah in building a strong and solid stand against Nkrumah. Both had returned to Ghana as heroes and were natural leaders of the post-coup era. Rivalry between them was inevitable; albeit regrettable. After all efforts to get both leaders to appear together as leaders of one party had failed, each of them formed his own political party.

The National Alliance of Liberals (N.A.L.) was formed by K.A. Gbedemah, following the lifting of the ban on politics and political life in April 1969. Well-organised, it derived its support chiefly from the Volta Region, the home territory of Gbedemah himself. Gbedemah threw into the organisation of his party, the same zeal, enthusiasm and dedication which he had shown during the early days of Nkrumah's party, the C.P.P., of which he was a founding member and a leading architect.

73

Dr Busia's party, the Progress Party, formed in about the same period, derived its support from the Akan areas, which constitute about 70 percent of the population. It attracted most of the country's elite, intellectuals, and a few of the ex-supporters of Nkrumah who felt that they had been let down by their previous leader. In the strongly anti-Nkrumah climate of the post-coup period any party which was remotely associated with Nkrumah's régime, did not stand any palpable chance of gaining public favour electorally. Unfortunately for N.A.L., quite a number of the former C.P.P. leaders, after their release from prison, threw in their lot with that party. Thus N.A.L.became associated in the public mind with the excesses, cruelty and corruption of the overthrown régime. The people wanted a change, and felt that to break with the political past would improve their sad economic and social position. Again, although many people had been arbitrarily detained by the Nkrumah régime, the majority of these were Akans, as opposed to the people from the Volta Region, the Ewes. The anti-Nkrumah people were thus more among the Akans than among the Ewes. This fact was later to be reflected in the election results.

There was also the general view of many people, both literate and illiterate, that although Gbedemah deserved all sympathy as a victim of Nkrumah's excesses himself, as the right-hand man of Nkrumah from 1949 right up to when he fell out of favour in 1964, he was very much responsible for some of the misdeeds of Nkrumah. This charge is valid, but, in my opinion, unfair as it does not give adequate credit to the strenuous efforts which Gbedemah made, both inside and outside the Government, to steer the Nkrumah régime from its chosen path of marxism, dictatorship and tyranny.

Although Gbedemah's party (N.A.L.) and Busia's (P.P.) were the two major post-coup parties, a host of minor, irrelevant parties also did crop up. Some were very limited in programme

74

and in support, being often limited to only the founder, his friends and relatives, and a handful of supporters in various parts of the country.

After over a decade without the taste of free, political activity, the lifting of the ban on politics in April 1969 led to the full blossoming of many minor, little parties, which differed very little in political programmes. They were chiefly tribal in origin and composition. Prominent among the minor parties were the United National Party (U.N.P.), the People's Action Party (P.A.P.) and the A.P.R.P. Entertaining rather utopian hopes of winning the election, these little parties soldiered on, but were not taken seriously by any but their few supporters.

After a long, and vigorous period of campaign, the General Elections were held on 29 August 1969. The military Government, true to its word, kept scrupulously out of the elections. However, it was becoming increasingly evident towards the last days preceding the election, that there was a rift in the Government in their unofficial attitude towards the parties. The Police Officers on the Council appeared to support N.A.L., while the soldiers on it were inclined to veer towards the progress party (P.P.). Thus once again the Akan versus Ewe political division in the country could be discerned in the military Government itself. The Police Officers were mostly Ewes, while the soldiers were mostly Akans. A further extension of this Akan v. Ewe confrontation could be detected from an incident which had happened in November 1968. Then, amid wild rumours that Nkrumah (in Guinea) was preparing an invasion force back to Ghana, the Police and Special Branch reported that they had unearthed a plot by the then Chief of Defence Staff (C.D.S.), head of the Army, Navy and Air Force, to bring Nkrumah back to Ghana, with Soviet aid and assistance. This incredible story brought the country almost to the point of hysteria. If indeed Nkrumah was coming back, presumably triumphantly, then what was going to happen to all the former Army Officers, Senior Police and Security Officers, Chiefs, top Civil Servants, Ministers and diplomats, who, as former supporters of Nkrumah, had become his most bitter denouncers and accusers since his fall? The public reaction to this incredible news was to re-affirm its loyalty and support to the military régime, and to howl for the death penalty for the alleged criminals. The C.D.S., Air Vice-Marshall Michael Otu, and his A.D.C. Lieutenant Kwapong (both Akans) were both accused of subversion, dismissed and arrested. Both strongly protested their innocence. Subsequently, they were cleared by a Commission of Enquiry, headed by a prominent Court of Appeal Judge. The Commission held that there was no evidence whatsoever in the allegations against the C.D.S. and his A.D.C. Meanwhile, both had already been dismissed, and it was the incoming administration of Dr Busia which re-instated them. So ended the mysterious story of Ghana's equivalent of the "Dreyfus Affair". The latter generated nationwide passions in France, and was motivated by anti-semitism. The "Otu Affair", in Ghana, similarly generated strong emotions and passions on a national scale, and it was held by many intelligent Ghanaians that tribalism was behind it all, and that, from the beginning to the end, it was merely an attempt to dislodge an Akan Chief of the Armed Forces and replace him by an Ewe. Whether they were right or wrong is for history ultimately to judge.

Even as the preparations for the election due in August 1969 were going on apace, major differences among the members of the military Government refused to die out. In April 1969, with the whole country agog with enthusiasm for a return to civilian rule, the State Radio announced that the Head of State and Chairman of the N.L.C., General J.A. Ankrah, who had been Head of State since the Coup, had resigned, allegedly for accepting a bribe, to enhance his political chances in the country.

During the period he was Head of the military Government, Ankrah brought a large measure of peace and moderation to the deliberations of the National Liberation Council. As he was in retirement at the time of the coup, and had been invited by the coup leaders, Col. E.K. Kotoka and Major A.A. Afrifa, to head the new Government, and thus add respectability and maturity to it, effective power in the end, lay in the hands of Kotoka and Afrifa. With Kotoka having been killed in the short-lived, abortive coup of April 1967, led by Lieutenant Arthur, Afrifa thus remained the natural leader of the new administration. However, in seniority, the Police Chief Harlley, and Brigadier Ocran, were senior to Afrifa. Both for personal reasons, refused the Chairmanship of the N.L.C., and Afrifa became the new Head of State, after Ankrah. As he had never hidden his detestation of the Nkrumah régime and its marxist claims and policies, Afrifa's elevation gave a big moral boost to the anti-Nkrumah groups.

Moreover, as Afrifa saw it, the logic of the political situation needed the replacement of the military régime by a Government which was not only civilian and democratic, but also anti-Nkrumah. Otherwise, having fought and defeated the Nkrumah régime, he felt one could well end, through, possibly, the electoral process exploiting some of the people's political ignorance and immaturity, with a new Government which was pro-Nkrumah and anti-democracy. There was the personal interest of Afrifa, and other senior military officers serving the N.L.C. – should the new civilian Government be pro-Nkrumah, there was the possibility of it putting on trial for treason all the officers who had taken part in the coup which over-threw Nkrumah. On this issue both the military and Police officers in the military Government, agreed completely. The urgent need for the non-return to power of Nkrumah's party, or any political party deriving from it, was thus a generally-accepted principle both among the rulers and the ruled. The only question was who among the anti-Nkrumah groups should take over from the military régime. That was what the General Elections of 29 August 1969, were mainly about.

The elections were carefully and properly organised by the Electoral Commissioner and his staff, based in Accra. Each party had its symbol, and in each polling booth, a photograph of the candidate and his party symbol were attached to his box. To eliminate double voting and other electoral malpractices, each voter's name was checked against the electoral register, and after he had voted alone and secretly in the polling booth, his thumb was imprinted with indelible ink, which could not be rubbed easily for about two days at least. The elections were vigorously contested by all parties taking part. At stake were 140 Parliamentary seats. As these were the first free elections since the one in 1956, immediately preceeding Independence, the 1969 elections drew much public interest and attention. Having witnessed the comical elections of 1964, and 1965, the people were keen to register their unfettered, genuine electoral wishes. The 1964 referendum on the establishment of a one-party state, and the presidential election had registered an unbelievably high figure of a 90 percent vote of support. For the 1965 "elections", the C.P.P. went even one step further. 198 candidates were hand-picked by the Central Committee of the party and then they were declared as "unopposed", and therefore elected. Some had never visited the constituencies which they were expected to represent. It was the most ridiculous and money-wasting electoral exercise ever conducted in Ghana's history.

About 2,351,658 voters, in an estimated population of about 8 million, were registered. Of these about 1,493,371 voted. The turnout was thus 64 per cent, which was very high in the country, considering the communication and transport difficulties. As the adult population of the country in 1969 was

78

about $3\frac{1}{2}$ million, it means that those who registered were 2,351,658 out of $3\frac{1}{2}$ million. When eventually all the votes were in, the Progress Party, led by Dr Busia had won by a convincing majority. It won 105 out of the 140 seats, with Gbedemah's party (N.A.L.) winning 29, and others 6, including one Independent candidate, Harry Sawyer.

The table below shows the general distribution of seats, and how they were won.

Region	Seats	Progress	N.A.L.	Others
Ashanti	22	22	0	0
Brong-Ahafo	13	13	0	0
Central Region	15	15	0	0
Western	13	10	0	3
Eastern	22	18	4	0
Volta	16	2	14	0
Northern	14	9	5	0
Upper	16	13	3	0
Accra	9	3	3	3
TOTAL	140	105	29	3

Although the losing parties made minor public complaints, unconvincingly, about possible malpractices in the elections, the general view of many independent observers including foreign press-men and such astute and knowledgeable observers of the

Ghana scene and of the elections, such as Prof Dennis Austin, Prof of Government, Manchester University, England was that the elections were fair, properly-conducted, without any interference from any quarter. Having won 105 out of the 140 parliamentary seats, Dr Busia, as leader of the Progress Party, became the first Prime Minister of the second Republic of Ghana. He had won after many years of dogged opposition to tyranny, corruption, dictatorship, and marxism. Meanwhile, on 2 September 1969, a Presidential Commission was set up to replace the N.L.C. It consisted of A.A. Afrifa, as Chairman, the Head of the Police Force, J.W.K. Harlley, as Vice-Chairman, and Major-Gen A.K. Ocran, Acting Chief of Defence Staff.

On 1st October 1969, at a most memorable ceremony in State House, Accra, before an august gathering of Chiefs, diplomats, eminent citizens and visitors, Dr Kofi Abrefa Busia, was sworn in as the new Prime Minister of Ghana. The country had made the transformation from dictatorship to democratic, civilian rule smoothly and without a hitch. Among the dozens of African states under military rule in 1969, Ghana was the first and only country to have made the historic transition.

The credit for the handing over goes without question to the military officers in the Government at the time. Some, like Afrifa and Ocran, were at the very top. Some were in the regions as Commissioners (Governors). Some were in the State Corporations as Managing Directors or Managers. Some were Ambassadors. For them all and their friends, the return to civilian rule was a big blow personally. It meant a return to the hard and rigid life of the barracks, the foregoing of the usual perks and social prestige attendant on civilian offices of state. It meant "a loss of face", in one way or another. Yet for their love of democracy and freedom and justice these men were prepared to deny themselves all possible social and personal advantages for the general good of the country. Whatever might be the shortcomings and foibles of these people; whatever might be their personal ambitions and weaknesses, history would judge them well and kindly. When it comes to the crunch, it should be remembered that at the material moment in Ghana's history, if these men had refused to surrender power what could anyone have done? Nothing! Indeed when one reflects on the major sacrifice of the military officers of the post-coup period, one is tempted to repeat the famous words of Sir Winston Churchill in 1940 in Britain's hour of destiny: *"Never in the history of human conflict was so much owed by so many to so few."*

Unfortunately for Ghana, the handing over by the military to the civilians, which opened a historic epoch was not to last long. That was to be the fate of Ghana.

Chapter 6 – Seeds of Tragedy

If the immediate causes of the Revolution in Ghana can be discerned from the actions and policies which were pursued by the second military Government (1972-1979), the remote causes of that Revolution can be traced to the actions and policies of the post-coup civilian Government of Dr Busia and the events which took place in the period October 1969 – January 1972. In more than the literal sense the Busia Government was the cause of its own downfall. When it took over on 1 October 1969, the new civilian Government, like its military predecessor, took on all the international debts and liabilities of the country. Aware of its international and moral obligations, the Busia Government did the right thing by assuming responsibility for these debts. Moreover, it was rational to assume that any other course of action would have seriously jeopardised further credits and economic assistance from the West, to whom the bulk of these debts were owed.

Imports were very restricted, thus, leading to major shortages of essential food items and other urgently needed commodities. Due to the shortage of these goods, the few which were available were very expensive and hard to get; thereby occasioning a flourishing black-market trade. The cedi was non-convertible and it was illegal to take it out of the country. It therefore meant that there was a greater desire by many people to jettison the cedi for convertible currency, especially the British sterling and the U.S. dollar. In fact, at one time the situation had become so bad that the black-market rate of the cedi was one-fifth that of its official rate against the British pound or U.S. dollar or French franc.

Admittedly, the out-going military régime had tried to grapple with these economic problems, by devaluing the cedi, checking smuggling across the borders, and removing some of the restrictions on the economy, especially on the importation of essential food items and other similar commodities. As stated earlier they had also paid off some of Ghana's debts and borrowed more to finance food imports and the regular supply of drugs, spare parts, machinery and essential raw materials for the country's factories. But it should be remembered that the N.L.C. considered as its chief objective, the removal of the Nkrumah régime and the restoration of democracy. It considered itself wholly as a caretaker Government, which in the meantime had to do something about the economy to keep it from complete collapse before the real politicians took over. They never felt it their duty to undertake a drastic re-structuring of the economy, especially as it was anticipated all along that return to civilian rule was just round the corner.

The economic problems that faced the new Busia Government were enormous. High prices, high unemployment; scarcity of food, goods and essential services, and the continuous public clamour for more schools, colleges, free health facilities, subsidised transport, petrol, food, etc. The truth of the matter was that these demands for the benefits of the welfare-state had been in existence since the days of Independence in 1957. In fact, they stem from the advent of the Nkrumah Government into power in 1951. The socialist programmes of Nkrumah had catapulted him into office, and generally kept him there. The country could then afford to supply the people these welfare demands. When it was no longer possible to finance these programmes from the nation's own resources, due to the fall in prices of cocoa, timber, gold, etc., on the world market, Nkrumah had borrowed heavily to maintain these levels of welfare to keep the people if not happy, at least not too vociferous and boisterous. For, as Nkrumah often jokingly stated in private, and sometimes in public, there has never been a case of a country being taken to court and imprisoned for its debts!

When, however, towards 1964-65, no further external credits were available for Ghana's imports and other needs, the régime turned to the services of the Military Intelligence, Special Branch, and the well-paid party zealots to keep the people quiet, at least on the surface. As outlined in earlier chapters, the régime, to a large extent, succeeded in living in this self-created dream-world of calm, peace and success!

As long as the military régime remained in control of affairs, the demands of the public for more jobs, more houses, the benefits of the welfare-state, although persistent, were rather muted. Nobody wanted to upset the applecart. Nobody wanted to take up the cudgels against the men with arms. But when in October 1969, the return to civilian, democratic rule was effected, the people who had generally been rather quiet during the past three and a half years of military rule, felt bold enough to begin to express their demands more openly and publicly.

The press, although still owned and controlled by the State, were now free to a very large extent – certainly more than in any period of the country's history. Although in the period of military rule the press were relatively free, certainly far freer than under the previous régime, the very exigencies of the situation, i.e. military rule, meant that all editors and writers operated under an unwritten, self-imposed code of "censorship" for very obvious reasons. With the promulgation of the new Constitution for Ghana, real freedom was allowed, and all restrictions on the press, freedom of expression, religion, movement, association, disappeared overnight.

The Busia Government had come into high office with the excited acclamations of the public that it was the party best fitted to bring democratic civilian rule real "freedom and justice" (the nation's motto) to the whole country. The leader's impeccable political and personal credentials as an avowed, pro-Western liberal democrat were well known and fully established. As a matter of fact, one of the major reasons for the tremendous success of the Progress Party at the General Elections in August 1969, was the generally-held belief in the whole country, that with his long pro-British and pro-West connections and contacts, he would be more successful in getting more aid, economic assistance and external credits for Ghana than could be obtained by another leader who did not have the same political and academic contacts in the West which Dr Busia had.

With the economic and social demands and expectations of the masses at a very high level, and with most people looking on Dr K.A. Busia as Ghana's new hope, the country was launched on democratic, civilian rule on 1 October 1969. The new Prime Minister first of all chose a Cabinet, which represented all the regions and tribes of the country, except the Volta Region, where the Government Party had won no seats at the General Elections. The Cabinet contained some of the best brains in the country. It was made up of men like J.H. Mensah, an internationally-known economist; R.A. Quashie, an experienced industrialist and ex-diplomat; Victor Owusu, a veteran lawyer, politician and economist; Kwesi Lamptey, Paa Willie, S.D. Dombo and others. They were men whose suffering and sacrifice for democracy and liberalism were well-known. The public dubbed the Government "the country's best brains", and so indeed they were. The public expected a lot from them.

Dr Busia and his Government, once sworn into office, set out relentlessly to deal with the grave economic problems of the country. The advice and financial assistance of the I.M.F., the World Bank were sought. High-powered delegations led by J.H. Mensah, as Finance Minister, were sent out to go to the

West, to negotiate the re-scheduling of Ghana's immense debts, estimated at about one billion U.S. dollars. The Prime Minister himself paid a number of official visits to the U.S.A., Britain, West Germany and other Western European countries delivering the fresh message of friendship and co-operation with the West, and pleading for greater economic assistance to Ghana in the form of softer loan terms, longer debt repayment periods, direct grants and the supply of machinery and expertise.

The trend towards liberalising the economy, which had been initiated under the military régime, was continued. Further restrictions on the economy were removed, and the rigid application of import controls was relaxed. Dr Busia, by retaining in office all the civilian Commissioners (Ministers) who served in the military régime and had, as members of his political party, fought and won seats in the elections, ensured continuity of policy between the military régime and its successor. R.A. Quashie, Minister of Trade and Tourism, and J.H. Mensah, Finance Minister, retained the same offices under the civilian government as they held under the military Government. Victor Owusu, Attorney-General in the military régime became Foreign Minister. A few others who held posts under the N.L.C. came to hold Ministerial positions in the new Government. It was thus obvious to all that the Government, with the full support of the press and the public, were determined to maintain the pro-West, pro-British image and stance of the military régime.

While importing more food items, spare parts, essential drugs and machinery to keep the public happy, the Government, especially its leader, constantly reminded the public of the grave economic position of the country; the need for sacrifice, and belt-tightening by all, and the unpleasant and hard days that lay ahead.

Dr Busia often in public speeches told his audience that the country's economy was gravely sick, and needed to be given "very unpalatable and strong medicine", which was the only way to cure the patient. All this made sense to the people, who heartily welcomed Dr Busia wherever he went with his message.

The first Budget of the Busia Government, was generally a continuation of the last budget of the N.L.C. Greater emphasis on private enterprise, less emphasis on state intervention, greater liberalization of the import controls; encouragement of foreign investors – these were among the salient features of the new economic policy of the new, civilian Government. The first budget statement of the Busia Government showed the new trends in the Government's economic thinking – a positive move away from state intervention in the economy.

Unfortunately, as the Government implemented its economic programmes, duly thought out as being in the nation's best interests, the Government's popularity began to dwindle. What was happening was that as the Government's economic policies began to bite, it caused immense economic and financial havoc on the very centres of electoral power, which only a few months before had enthusiastically voted for the Progress Party, and therefore, were legitimately expecting the appropriate rewards. What then were the centres of power which had made Busia's accession to his position possible?

First there were the farmers. Overwhelmingly, the rural areas where 70-80 per cent of the populations live, mainly as farmers and fishermen, had voted for the Progress Party, as the party for the rural folk. They had been promised increase in the prices of cocoa and other cash-crops and the supply of fertilizers, fishing nets and machines at heavily subsidized prices. The Busia Government kept its promise. The necessary price rise to farmers for their produce was effected. But with the world-wide inflation and recession from 1970 it meant that the rural folk, like the rest of the population, were badly hit by the high inflation and the exhorbitant cost of basic consumer items such as salt, imported food, grass-mats, kerosene lamps and similar items. Admittedly, unlike the C.P.P. days, the goods were available, but only their prices were too high for the ordinary farmer of fisherman, despite the Government's price subsidies. Thus from 1970 the rural folk were gradually being disillusioned, although the Government still spent more on them than had previously been done by any other Government, civilian or military. As time went on, and the conomic hardships to them became more severe, the farmers began to constitute a potential aggrieved group.

Secondly, the Armed Forces had been one of the main supporters of the Busia party at the time of the election. They and the Police, in order to allow them time to supervise the elections and check any fiddling or other election malpractices, had been allowed to vote a few days earlier than the General Election date of 29 August 1969. They had voted over-whelmingly for the Progress Party as the figures subsequently released were to show. Indeed about 65 per cent had voted for the party, and about 30 per cent for the opposition groups, thus reflecting almost accurately the general voting pattern among the civilians. Naturally, they were expecting high hopes from the new Government, in the form of improved conditions of service, revised pay, allowances etc. In fact, it is well worth remembering that one of the major reasons which was given by the Army for the 1966 coup against Nkrumah was the general deterioration in the service conditions of the Armed Forces personnel during the Nkrumah régime. Consequently when, as a result of its first and, especially the second budget, the Busia Government, as part of the programme of nation-wide belt-tightening, delved into the privileges of the armed forces, the latter also began to join the growing group of the malcontents and the disillusioned. The Busia Government for the first time in

Ghana's history asked the Armed Forces to make economic sacrifices. Their free rent, free water, free electricity and other allowances were stopped. These cuts affected all the armed forces, but especially so the officers. They lost also, like the senior civil servants, their car maintenance allowances, which in many cases were enough to cover the monthly loan repayments on the cars.

Thirdly, the powerful civil servants were also touched. It was part of the service conditions of the senior civil servants to be provided with beautifully furnished houses or bungalows by the State at very nominal rents, which did not in anyway reflect the prevailing economic rents in the country. This privilege had been taken for granted since the days of British rule. In fact the whole system of subsidized accommodation for senior civil servants was started by the British Colonial administration for very good reasons. At the time when the British took over the administration of Ghana as a colony, there were no suitable houses for the British doctors, engineers and administrators who were arriving from Britain. The colonial Government, therefore, built for them houses (generally in the suburbs away from local population) which the British officers could occupy.

As more Ghanaians entered the civil service as graduates, they and the public demanded that the first few Ghanaians who were fortunate enough to hold any of these "graduate" or "European" posts, should be given the same rights and privileges as the Europeans who occupied them. Indeed, the issue of Africans holding "European posts" being treated as Europeans by the colonial administration, was one of the major bones of contention in the mid-1940s during the struggle for independence. Ultimately, the colonial administration gave in and accorded the same privileges to the Ghanaians as to the British civil servants working in Ghana. These privileges, apart from similar subsidized accommodation, included a three month leave or holidays in the U.K. every eighteen months, with fares for wife and up to four children paid by the State. They also included the grant of an interest-free loan to purchase a car (with repayments spread over 3-5 years) and the award of a generous car maintenance allowance.

Right up to 1951, when Nkrumah's party came into office, the scheme outlined above worked very well, for there were not in any case more than a handful of Africans holding any of these senior positions. After independence in March 1957, when many of the British civil servants left, after collecting their agreed emoluments and gratuities, the whole civil service was Africanised and the financial burden of the scheme was becoming more and more acute. How dare any post-independence African Government deprive the senior civil service of the perks, privileges and other conditions of service which had been granted them by the British after a considerable struggle, and had become accepted by subsequent Governments as part of the overall civil service system?

Consequently, although Nkrumah's régime and the succeeding military régime, periodically made public references to the need for removing or curtailing these privileges, nothing was done about them. As a matter of fact, with every salary review, the very same allowances and perks were increased or improved upon to keep up with rising cost of living and inflation.

However, more and more astute observers of the national scene were beginning to question the wisdom of the whole scheme and its deleterious effect on the national economy. Such thinking was prompted, and buttressed, by the fact that it was known that such a scheme did not exist in Britain, the mother-country itself, whose ideals and way of life the new nation was being modelled on. The whole trouble was that although there were valid arguments for scrapping the system, it had become so ingrained and accepted by all that it had become politically unwise to change it. Besides, many of the critics of the scheme were also beneficiaries of its existence and stood to lose heavily if it were to be removed. This was the dilemna that faced the Busia Government in 1970.

Having the courage of its convictions, the Government, in one stroke, abolished the car maintenance allowance, drastically reduced the mileage allowance, raised the nominal rent of 10 per cent of occupant's salary for the Government bungalows to 20 per cent and did away with a host of perks and privileges for the Army and the Civil Servants. Consequently, the massive support and goodwill for the Government which existed among the groups at the time it came into office suddenly evaporated. The Government was now on the defensive, and naturally the Opposition group (N.A.L.) gloating over the situation, fully exploited it to the maximum. The Government's discomfiture and embarrassment had come as a boon to the Opposition's sagging fortunes.

Fourthly, even the business community who had enthusiastically financed and supported the Progress Party during the elections, did not escape the severe sacrifices for the nation, which the new Government was asking. Before the Governments' arrival on the scene, the existence of rigid import controls, meant that businessmen with political clout, who could manage to get import licences for specific items, could make huge profits on them, despite the price control scheme which was never seriously implemented and operated. The Progress Party, being anti-Nkrumah in origin and policy, was acceptable to businessmen who supported it to victory, and expected a new economic climate which would enhance private enterprise. To some extent, a very large extent, the new Government fulfilled these expectations. Certain restrictions on the economy were removed. A new multi-million cedi Government loan scheme was launched to assist small Ghanaian businessmen to buy foreign businesses or to start from scratch. Favourable interest rates were granted by this organisation. And the banks were encouraged to help businessmen generally.

However, the Government felt that it was right to lift import restrictions in order to free the economy, and also to cut deeply into the rampant bribery and corruption involved in the implementation of import controls. Since possession of an import licence literally meant the freedom to print money, a number of businessmen went out of their way to corrupt some of the civil servants who were involved in the granting of import licences. The whole import licence system was the source of fraudulent practices and corruption on a gigantic scale, and the Progress Government was completely justified in its determined efforts to scrap it and return to a limited free market economy. But this very action meant that the businessmen (many of whom had supported the Government) stood to lose very badly. In some cases, profits were severly curtailed while a few businesses collapsed. Over-riding the fears and financial losses of its businessmen-supporters, the Government stuck to its guns at the peril of losing the moral and financial support of the local and foreign (chiefly Lebanese and Indian) businessmen.

Inspired by the country's best interests, the new Government did not spare even its favourite sons, the University students who constituted the fifth political base of the party. During the election compaign, the overwhelming majority of the students had supported the party, canvassed for it and campaigned vigorously for its victory at the polls. But, if there must be equity in suffering then how could one seriously exclude the students from the widespread austerity measures? The Government had promised in its manifesto to provide more elementary and secondary education opportunities in the country, especially in the rural areas. To raise more funds for the scheme it introduced a new law whereby University education would no longer be free, but that the students, following the American pattern, would be granted interest-free loans to be repaid when they completed their courses and were employed. The universities, three of them in all, were asked to cut down their overall expenditure by introducing the non-residential campus system, as opposed to the more expensive residential system, which was a considerable drain on the economy. Thus, another political prop of the Government was removed by the introduction of this prudent, financial measure, and student demonstrations followed. The students had become overnight vitriolic critics and opponents of the new Government.

Next the *Trade Unions* who, under Nkrumah had become an integral wing of the ruling party, C.P.P. Under the military régime, they had regained their independence and freedom, but were ideologically more in tune with the C.P.P., than the Progress Party. Consequently, when in 1971, the T.U.C. organised a series of protests and demonstrations against the Government's austerity measures, there was a feeling that some of their leaders were trying to exploit the economic situation to usher in a marxist state, reminiscent of the Nkrumah days. Parliament consequently passed legislation banning the T.U.C.!

Determined as it was to put the national interest first, the Busia Government tackled a major political problem which had been ignored by previous Ghana Governments. For a number of years many Ghanaians had been unhappy about the prominent role played in local commerce and trade by Lebanese and Indians who owned a lot of small shops. In practically all these cases they had arrived in the country without bringing in any foreign exchange. By borrowing from the local banks and financial institutions, they had prospered in commerce to the disadvantage of the local Ghanaians. Rumours were rife that Ghanaian bank managers preferred to give loans and overdraft facilities to Lebanese and Indians because of bribes and commissions which the businessmen gave the banks which their Ghanaian compatriots were not prepared to do. The fact that some of these bank officials were known publicly to be very cosy with these foreigners, plus the fact that some of them upon retirement, took up senior positions in businesses which had been partly financed by the banks gave much credence to these rumours and stories.

Many Ghanaians still remembered vividly that in the early days of struggle for Independence (1948-1950) against the British colonial administration, the Lebanese and Indians had, unashamedly, sided with the British, joining the anti-riot squads with long truncheons to beat the Africans demonstrating for Independence. In addition to all this, there was the feeling of many Ghanaians that the Indians and Lebanese, unlike the West Europeans and Americans, were making no meaningful contribution to the country's development and progress.

While people understood Ghana's dependence on the West for loans, economic assistance, and educational facilities, and, therefore, the need to be accommodating as much as possible towards them, they could not see any clear and direct benefits which they derived from the thousands of Lebanese and Indians in the country, who ran shops and businesses that could easily be undertaken by Ghanaians. Frequent press reports of financial malpractices by some of these people, including smuggling money out the country (of course, with the connivance and collusion of Ghanaians) did not help matters very much.

The Busia Government in 1970 brought in legislation whereby certain categories of jobs and businesses were designated only for Ghanaians. The Government's popularity shot up with the Ghanaian public, as a result of this legislation and many Ghanaians were able to *buy* businesses from the Lebanese and Indians. To be fair, the previous military régime

(1969) had brought in a decree requesting the registration of all aliens, and the repatriation of all those in the country without valid immigration papers. The decree also excluded non-Ghanaians from certain enterprises and businesses. But the decree was never enforced by the military régime, and it became the lot of the succeeding Progress Government not only to enforce it, but to bring into effect complementary, supporting legislation.

Businessmen from the West were not very bothered by these restrictions, as they were not generally affected. Unfortunately, in the implementation of these new laws the Busia administration took on more than it could cope with. It included in the exercise all Africans, including those from Nigeria, Liberia and the surrounding African States, many of whom were engaged in local trade on a minor scale, but nation-wide. Some of these had inter-married with the locals, or had been in the country for many years. The repatriation of these people and others on a massive scale, for which the administration did not have the requisite experience or logistic support, remains one of the few dark spots in the glorious record of that administration. Instead of concentrating on the bad Lebanese and Indians, who although few, did a collossal damage to the country's economy through over-invoicing, under-invoicing, profiteering, black-market-eering and currency smuggling, the Busia Government rather concentrated on the non-Ghanaian Africans, who were numerous and, because they looked like Ghanaians, were very difficult to identify. Later on, the Prime Minister personally told me in an interview in his office in the Castle, Accra, in 1971, that the whole implementation of the scheme had been botched up and major mistakes had been made.

Thus by 1971, all the surrounding African states were at loggerheads with the Ghana Government over the forced repatriation of their citizens. The Lebanese and Indian businessmen, those ejected, and those still remaining, had no love for the Progress Government. And the common-law wives, mistresses and household staffs and employees of those of them who had left were pouring curses on the Government. Once again the Busia Government had, with lofty intentions, done the right thing in the wrong way. The prominent intervention of Lebanese and Indians in Ghanaian commerce was thus, unsurprisingly, one of the major causes of the Revolution in 1979.

Indeed, it is perfectly valid to say that the record of the Busia Government was a whole catalogue of one botched up exercise after another, each undertaken with the best of motives and with the highest interests of the nation in mind. Looking back, it is very painful to reflect on the mistakes in strategy and public relations which helped to ruin the image of the best Government that Ghana has ever had. While the Government was being forced to implement one austerity measure after another, it took on the political front actions which were counter-productive and very damaging to its political interests. I believe that most of these rather unhelpful political actions by the Progress Government might have been induced by the opposition groups to inveigle the Government into action in an anti-democratic, illiberal way, thus making nonsense of its impeccable liberal background and reputation.

First of all, the Leader of the Opposition, K.A. Gbedemah, a former collaborator of Busia in exile, who had won a parliamentary seat himself, was unseated from Parliament by his Progress Party opponents through legal proceedings based on Article 71 of the new Constitution. This article excluded from Parliament all persons against whom adverse findings had been made by a Committee or Commission of Enquiry. As Gbedemah had been so reported upon by one of the commissions after Nkrumah's fall, the High Court ruled against his seat in Parliament. He, therefore, had to leave Parliament, for the benefit of the Progress candidate.

Secondly, early in 1970, the Government, acting on the letter of the new Constitution, which allowed it not to re-appoint certain persons if it did not so wish, dismissed 568 members of the civil service. One of the victims of the dismissal exercise, E.K. Sallah, a manager of the State Trading Corporation, an Ewe, challenged his dismissal in the Supreme Court. After the Attorney-General's objection to the panel had been overruled by a 4:1 majority, Sallah won his case that he had been wrongfully dismissed. The verdict was 3:1 in his favour, with one abstention. Instead of the matter ending there quietly, it became blown out of all proportion by the press and local media agents. The Prime Minister's public radio and television attack on the judgement of the Supreme Court left a bitter taste in the mouths of all those who looked on the Progress Government as that of "the best men" in the country, the most enlightened.

But unlike Dr Nkrumah in similar circumstances in 1963, Dr Busia confined his actions to a public blast of the judiciary, and did not sack the Court concerned. Still, for a democratic, liberal, enlightened Government, the little that Busia did was to hang like a stinking albatross round the neck of his Government, and future ones. Indeed, followers of Dr Busia are still paying politically for the consequences of this dismissal exercise, popularly known in Ghana as "*Apollo 568*". Apart from the counter-productive nature of the exercise in political terms, it also had the dangerous side-effects that it alienated a number of persons, strong supporters of the party, who by error, had been included in the exercise! Assuming that by the extended family system each educated Ghanaian is directly responsible for at least twenty persons it means that overnight the administration, apart form the immediate 568 victims of the exercise, had alienated the active support of at least 568 x 20 people, i.e. over 11,360. This is collossal in a voting population of about

1,493,371. Whatever the administrative advantages of the exercise, looking back, it is evident that the loser was the Busia Government itself.

Thirdly, although it is on record that the Busia Government did not detain or imprison arbitrarily a single soul, a distinction which it holds among all the Governments in Ghana before and after Independence, its treatment of the then Editor of the Daily Graphic, Cameron Duodu, was not in confirmity with the Government's own liberal precepts. At a press conference in 1970 at his office in the Castle in Accra, Dr Busia was asked an impromptu question on Apartheid in South Africa. Replying to the question, and emphasizing Ghana's opposition to Apartheid and racial discrimination, he also stated that he believed in the need for a dialogue between South Africa and other African States, towards impressing on South Africa the dangers of Apartheid.

Suddenly the Dialogue issue became a major political affair, with the Prime Minister being cast in the role of a renegade, African leader, unashamedly prepared to do a deal with South Africa. The Opposition press took up the issue and pressed home their advantage. Over the whole nation it appeared that nobody, apart from the Prime Minister himself, supported "Dialogue" as it came to be called. On radio and television all the discussions were against "Dialogue", and even the Foreign Minister, Victor Owusu, was known to be opposed to it, as were other members of the Government, although it was too embarrassing for them to say so in public. Only the Minister of Information came on television to defend "Dialogue", which had within a short period become synonymous with betrayal of the African. The State papers were equally unenthusiastic about it. The most vociferous opponent among the press was the editor of the largest daily newspaper, the Daily Graphic. In a series of editorials, the editor – himself a strong supporter of the

99

Government, made a rational and convincing case against "Dialogue". Suddenly in 1971, the editor was dismissed. Even his friendship with the then Finance Minister, was unable to save him. Cameron Duodu's removal made him a national hero, for a lot of people agreed with him. Although dismissed, he was not arrested or harrassed in any way by the Government, and carried on happily with his job as a writer and Ghana correspondent for a number of British and American papers.

It is worth recording that rumours then that Dr Busia had made his statement on "Dialogue" because he had received funds for the 1969 elections from South Africa, through Ivory Coast (another supporter of "Dialogue"), are mere suspicious speculations, which have no incontrovertible factual basis whatsoever. The statement by Busia, and his dogged public and private defence of his stand, when even his own Cabinet evidently had deserted him, was very much in consonance with his peaceful and quiet nature and his utmost dedication to Christian morality, deriving from his deep-seated Methodist background. It is regrettable that in the circumstances his stand made him appear as a friend of South Africa.

Other infractions of the liberal tradition and image of the Busia Government were the passing of legislation disallowing any publicity about Nkrumah – his principles, ideas, and policies. There was genuine fear in 1970-71 that Nkrumah, based in Guinea, might launch a return to power, by initially trying to destabilize the State through the press, old contacts, the workers and market-women. Retrospectively, such fear was minimal and obviously it was an over-reaction on the part of the Government to go in for such undemocratic piece of legislation, although the law was never seriously implemented and no prosecutions under it ever took place.

Equally unnecessary was the law which was passed to protect the Prime Mininster from insults, rumours and abuse. Although, it was possible that political opponents were probably behind the spate of anti-Busia demonstrations and protests in 1970-71, including stone-throwing against the Prime Minister in Accra, the Busia Government, with its massive parliamentary majority (105 out of 140 seats), and its generally wide support in the whole country, should have risen above these minor, irrelevant irritations and annoyances, instead of being tempted to move against them by resort to rather harsh and illiberal laws.

Yet, when all is said and done, even these minor deviations from the smooth path of freedom and democratic rule, were, in no way, a threat to the fundamentals of democracy as understood in America or Western Europe. At no time, despite all the provocations of the opposition groups, did the Busia Administration contemplate mass arrests of opponents, their harrassment or detention. Nor was it ever contemplated to stay in office ad infinitum, by declaring a one-party state or postponing elections or undermining the Constitution. What the Busia Government did wrong on the economic front was always well-intentioned and loftily-motivated, but wrongly executed and badly-timed. On the political front, an unjustified insecurity in its future, despite its overall popularity, made it pass a few anti-democratic laws. Looking back, all those who participated in the exercise, including this author, must feel very remorseful.

With the country in the economic and political state as outlined in this chapter, with unemployment high, cost of living rising, inflation soaring, and the people demanding more and more benefits, the Government suffered another blow. The world prices of cocoa, timber and gold suffered a marked fall. The costs of imports were rising rapidly. The world recession of the early 70's and the oil crises, occasioned by the sudden rise in oil prices by the oil-exporting states, contributed to the economic problems of Ghana. The catalogue of economic problems and dire circumstances led the Busia government to make two major moves which brought matters to a head.

In the July 1971 Budget the Government, apart from touching on the privileges of the Armed Forces, made a considerable cut in the vote for the Armed Forces. At that time the Chief of Defence Staff was a renowned air-foirce officer, Air Vice-Marshall M.S.Otu, who had been reinstated as Chief of Defence Staff (C.D.S.) following the notorious "Otu Affair", reminiscent of the "Dreyfus Affair". Otu was known to be professionally first-class, and a strong supporter of the Busia Government. But even he found it intolerable to run the Armed Forces on the new budget appropriations. Giving that as his reason, he resigned and retired. Events then began to move very fast. Following the resignation of Otu, the command of the Armed Forces had to be re-organised. The then Army Commander, Major-General Addo, became the new C.D.S., and to replace him as Army Commander, the Brigade Commander in the South (which includes Accra), Brigadier Twum-Barima was appointed. The position of Brigadier Commander for the South, thus became vacant.

The most senior and eligible officer for the post was Brigadier Asare. But he was known to be a close friend of the former Foreign Minister, later Attorney-General, Victor Owusu. His opposition to "Dialogue" was well-known, and many in the party and in the country, felt that he would be a more dynamic leader than the Prime Minister himself. There was no love lost between the two men. As such, when in the Cabinet and during party discussions of the appointment of the first Brigade commander, Victor Owusu, consistently supported the appointment of Asare, his whole stand was looked upon with grave suspicion. It was hinted that perhaps in his golf-sessions with Asare, he was in cahoots with him to sponsor his appointment and then capture high office, after a coup executed by Asare.

The 1966 coup had shown that no coup in Ghana could

succeed without the support of the southen command. Moreover, Asare, being a Fanti, and not Ashanti, did not help his cause much in a Government which was predominantly Ashanti-orientated and influenced. The fact that Victor Owusu is an Ashanti and not a Fanti made his motives more suspect. An Ashanti-Fanti axis would command very likely the support of the Akans (i.e. Ashantis and Fantis) who constitute about 70 per cent of the population.

Lt. Col. I.K. Acheampong, who was the most junior among the three possible candidates for the command, had a lot of advantages on his side. He was an Ashanti and was known to be a strong supporter of the Progress Party. He was even known to have carried openly a party card, against military regulations. He made no secret of his support of the Government, which was strongly based in Ashanti. Furthermore, he had a few powerful Ashanti friends in the Cabinet and among the junior ministers, whom he canvassed privately. They saw him as the man with the best credentials for the post, especially as far as loyalty to the Government was concerned. He was known to have told some of these friends many times that he would shed his blood, if need be, to defend the Busia Government. He had had a chequered career in the Army, which he had joined as a private. His promotion from lieutenant-colonel to colonel had got stuck for many years over alleged problems of chronic indebtedness, inefficiency, matrimonial problems, drunkenness and woman-ising on an impressive scale.

After the fall of the Nkrumah régime, Acheampong had served briefly (1968-69) as Regional Commissioner (i.e. Governor) in the Western Region, thus tasting political power for the first time in his life. This period had been followed by a spell in the U.S.A. for a graduate military course. He also served as President of a military tribunal in the West Indies. In 1970 he had returned to Ghana, after these experiences, which must have had a considerable impact on him. For a man whose formal education was limited to the Commercial College at Agona Swedru; who was not born with a silver spoon in his mouth, Acheampong by 1970, at the age of forty years had gone very far. But not far enough from his point of view. Following the continuous wrangling in the party and Government over the appointment of the Commander, First Infantry Brigade, (i.e. the Southern Command) Lt. Col. I.K. Acheampong, was jumped over his senior colleagues and given the appointment. This move made sense, although obviously it had rather tribal overtones. After all the Government was predominantly Ashanti-inspired, financed and led.

Since the first coup in February 1966, the conventional wisdom in political circles in Ghana had it that the next coup, if any, would come from among the Ewes, the people in the Volta Region, from which district the ruling party had not won any parliamentary seats in the 1969 elections. Ironically, quite a number of the senior officers in the Armed forces at the time the Progress Government took over in October 1969, were Ewes. They included the commanders of the Air Force, Navy, and a few senior officers in direct command of troops. That the first coup had been led by an Ewe, E.K. Kotoka, must have added, naturally, to the nervousness of the Government. Thus it was rational to expect the next coup-strike, if any, to come from the Volta Region. And against such a possible strike, it was logical and rational to count on Ashanti officers. Although, since the coup in 1972, the Busia Government has been accused of naivety, stupidity and crass innocence of human nature, it must be remembered that given the political situation prevailing at the time (1970-71), Acheampong's appointment appeared perfectly rational.

A few days after his appointment there were rumours that a coup was imminent, being organised by I.K. Acheampong.

These rumours emanated from the military units based in HO in the Volta Region and also from the military units based in Burma Camp, the chief military barracks, in Accra. Unreasonable as these rumours appeared, the National Security Committee set to investigate them. Indeed, a few days before these secret investigations, a prominent chief, who held the rank of a junior minister, had personally gone to the Castle (the seat of Government) in Accra and informed the Prime Minister of the direct evidence which he had received from a soldier in HO who claimed to be privy to the coup. The Prime Minister, who was not very well, and was scheduled to leave soon for an eye-operation (frequently postponed, due to official work) in London, was naturally incredulous about this news. This was not surprising. For since taking office on 1 October 1969, there had been so many rumours of coups, counter-coups, impending coups and abortive coups, that he must have resigned himself to these rumours. Indeed, he is alleged to have reacted to the effect that if having been properly and democratically elected as the Prime Minister, it was the will of God that he should be removed by a coup so soon after he had been in office, then there was nothing he could do about it. He had then been in office for only 26 months, and neither he nor many members of the Government, had even completed the traditional, protocol visits to the regions, ministries and departments, let alone familiarize themselves fully with all the problems of the country and its people.

It was in this general frame of mind that the security services began to investigate the rumour, in early January 1972, that a coup was being planned by Lt. Col. I.K. Acheampong. The sources of the rumour were both military, and civilian. The Director of Military Intelligence, Col. Joshua Hamidu, after a careful investigation of the rumour, presented his report to the National Security Committee. I am reliably informed that the report, a masterly and highly professional analysis of the situation, concluded that Acheampong, being an Ashanti, a prominent party-supporter, who had just been recently given the post over others senior to him and just been promoted in consonance with his new command to the rank of a full colonel, could simply not be planning any coup. In effect, that this rumour, like all others before it, was a piece of red-herring or was artificially manufactured by certain aggrieved groups for their own interests.

Acheampong was thus exonerated – even though kept under surveillance to the extent that a day before he did strike he was playing an exciting game of tennis with the Director of Military Intelligence. Alas, by the time these rumours were checked, counter-checked and discounted, Acheampong's plans had gone too far to be withdrawn, even if he wished to do so. Indeed, he himself was to tell a group of officers, who were confidants of his, during a Christmas party at Accra in 1976, that when his long-awaited appointment and promotion came in early January 1972 he was at his wits' end what to do. He battled with his conscience endlessly whether to repay the Government which had just rewarded him with promotion and appointment by reneging on his plans, and in so doing deny himself of the highest office of state and also disappoint his co-conspirators who had gone rather far with the coup plans under his direction and leadership, or pursue the inglorious path of treachery which he had chosen.

Previous to the coup, according to the Head of Special Branch at the time, he had noticed peculiar and unusual changes in the guards responsible for the most strategic positions in Accra, namely the seat of Government, i.e. the Castle, Flagstaf House (the Army Headquarters), the Broadcasting House, the General Post Office, Airport and the Borders. Upon being questioned, the newly appointed brigade commander, Lt.Col. I.K. Acheampong gave what appeared to be fairly simple and reasonable explanations for the changes. He was, he allegedly stated, "merely making routine changes in command", for heightened effectiveness, to guard these sensitive installations. This story, by the head of Special Branch at the time of the coup, was told to all of us in prison at Ussher Fort, Accra on the night of our arrest on 13 January 1972. Indeed, the security services had defused or aborted 19 different attempts from October 1969 – January 1972!

The real significance of what Acheampong had done was to become evident when he did strike. By the new troop dispositions he had placed around these installations and centres of power, soldiers and officers specially loyal to him, who had been deployed so that there would be no need of his orders being challenged or countermanded when he struck.

Meanwhile, Lt. Col. I.K.Acheampong and his co-conspirators kept on with their coup plans, waiting all the time for the most auspicious hour to strike. Superficially the security of the State was in the safest hands. Despite the fact that the desperate economic state of the country had put the whole country in a state of agitation and tension, there was no indication that anybody could be grappling better with a near-hopeless economic situation and doing more for the nation. With all the constraints on the economy, the internal and external debts of the Administration (mostly inherited from the previous Administration), the fall in export prices, and the phenomenal rise in the cost of imports due to the world inflation, caused by the upshot of oil prices, the Busia Government, within the 27 months it was in office, provided relatively more water, medical, educational and transportation facilities for the people, especially those in the rural areas, than had been ever done by any Government within a similar period. It was unthinkable to suggest then that the people of Ghana would sit there aloof to watch the overthrow of such a Government.

Putting, as always, the best interests of the nation first, the Busia Government had, in late December 1971, acting on the advice of both prominent local and international economists and experts, devalued the local currency, the cedi, by 44 per cent. The nett effect of this much-needed economic remedy was to cause an immediate jump in the cost of living, and inflation, and lead to more unemployment, as some businesses and industries closed down. This, of course, heightened the unpopularity of the Government.

On January, 11 1972, the Prime Minister, Dr K.A.Busia, left Accra airport for London, for his long-overdue medical treatment for his diabetes and his eyes. At the airport to see him off, were as always, the top ministers, senior officials, diplomats, the new C.D.S., and other senior military commanders and officers, and the Police. In addition, were the usual large crowds of party supporters and sympathisers. Everything appeared normal and correct. Yet within a matter of hours, after Busia's departure from Accra, the improbable happened. Lt. Col. Ignatius Kutu Acheampong, Commander of the First Infantry Brigade, struck. Ghana's second coup had been launched.

Chapter 7 – Back To Military Rule

Acheampong took advantage of the Government's weakness and unpopularity in the country, following the introduction of the severe economic measures, which it had been forced to take for the country's good. As such, when he struck, the Government's national support was at its lowest ebb. The Government was at loggerheads with the Judiciary, the armed forces, the civil service, the students, the trade unionists, the Opposition, journalists (over "Dialogue") and indeed with every major centre of organised power in the land. The businessmen, with the money and necessary power that goes with it, were also in arms. Nothing seemed to be going right for the Government.

It was in such a state of chaos and disillusionment that Acheampong announced to a stunned nation that once again the Army had stepped in to clear "the mess" created by the politicians. At dawn on 12 January 1972, he put his secret, treacherous plan into operation. All the roads to and from the capital were blocked. The telephone system for the military barracks, Burma Camp, was disconnected and he ordered the arrest of senior military officers, Ministers, and the Acting Prime Minister, Kwesi Lamptey. As all the Ministers and top party officials were guarded by military personnel, this was the easiest part of the exercise.

Meanwhile, as news of the coup flashed through Accra by the grape-vine, and through the walkie-talkie system of the military and the security services, an emergency meeting of the National Security Committee was summoned to the Castle. The members of the committee who had not been arrested attended, and immediately contacted the commander responsible for the security of Accra, who was no other man than Lt. Col. I.K.Acheampong. For up till this time, although there was evidence of troop movements, nobody knew for certain who was responsible or who was organising the coup or revolt. After much difficulty, the National Security Committee, meeting in the Castle, established contact with Acheampong by walkie-talkie, using the emergency wavelengths and codes. Acheampong claimed at first to know nothing of the attempted coup, but promised to take immediate, "crisis-action" to crush it. The security committee had previously learnt from a loyal soldier that a cache of ammunitions had been stolen from one of the military centres, Teshie, during the night of 12 January 1972. He had run the six mile journey to tell his tale to alert a member of the Security Committee whom he knew. While the Security Committee was meeting in the Castle, contacting the Party General Secretary, leading members of the Government and the Police Chief, Acheampong was busily executing his plans to capture power, whilst ostensibly "crushing" the attempted coup.

After a rather unusual and inexplicable delay, while the weary members of the Committee waited, reviewing contingency plans and possible alternatives should the coup succeed, they eventually contacted Acheampong again. He was to inform them that he had caught some of the trouble-makers and was on his way to the Castle with them! That was excellent news, which must have lowered the blood-pressure of all those loyal and dedicated persons engaged in the life-and-death struggle to save democracy, and law and order in Ghana. While these good men were waiting for Acheampong, they heard on their walkie-talkies, a mysterious voice say, vaguely "put on the air-conditioner, stop, stop!" or words to that effect . Suddenly to their shock and incredibility they heard on the state radio, at about 5.30 am of 13 January, 1972, "I am Lt. Col. I.K. Acheampong . . ." That none of these persons on the committee did not get a heart attack on hearing the voice and its message remains a mystery. With the game lost, betrayed by their own man, the so-called "pure Ashanti", the Security Committee still did not give up. They tried to mobilise popular, mass-support through the well-known and indefatigable General-Secretary of the party, B.J.da Rocha, and others, but alas, it was too late. Meanwhile, the Head of the Police Force, an experienced and respected barrister, and former ambassador, quickly mobilised his forces, and sent a small detachment of armed police in armoured personnel vehicles to the Broadcasting House. These were quickly and easily disarmed by the troops of Acheampong.

The Chief of Defence Staff, Major-General Addo, surprised as all others were by the brigade commander's treacherous move, did everything humanly possible to organise an effective opposition and resistance to the revolt. But again, time was not on his side. Indeed, he was on his way to Tema to seek more troop-support when he was overpowered. Similar courage and inventiveness were shown by the Army Commander, Brigadier Twum-Barima and the Director of Military Intelligence, Col. Joshua Hamidu, both of whom point-blank refused to give in and co-operate with treachery and disloyalty. But by the time they knew of Acheampong's move, it was so late that nothing effective to neutralise it could be done. The aggressors had the advantage of Surprise and Time on their side, and this their opponents in the military knew only too well their significance.

The coup was ironically being executed by the very man responsible for the safety of Accra, who had the emergency, contingency plans of the country's security in his very hands. To cap it all, he had in the conspiracy the most heavily armed and best equipped unit in the Ghana Army, namely the Recce régiment based in Accra. Also on his side was the next in command of the battalion in Tema, near Accra, who had, like his other conspirators, immediately arrested all their superior

111

officers who did not support the coup, thus incapacitating them. It was touch and go whether Acheampong would succeed while these arrests were going on. The military units in Takoradi, Kumasi, HO and Tamale, remained aloof in their barracks. Like their senior colleagues and comrades in Accra, they had been overtaken by events and were not sure of the outcome. Also as there did not, unlike the first coup (1966) appear to be any justification for this one, it would appear imprudent in their viewpoint, to throw their lot in a major gamble, which had all the signs of being popularly unwelcome and likely to fail; with disastrous consequences for all who had supported or participated in it.

Consequently, right up to about 4 pm on 13 January, 1972, the appeals of Acheampong for support from other units were completely ignored. Excitedly, in his messages to the different units and their officers, soliciting their support, he promised them massive promotions, major improved service conditions, and the scrapping of all the financial restrictions which the Busia Government had placed on them and their life-style. At first these units would not budge. They withheld their support. However, by not moving against him, they indirectly gave him time to consolidate his forces and power. Indeed, all that he was pleading for was that if they would not be with him, at least, they should not be against him.

In the first coup, the arrests of Ministers had been effected by the Police, as ordered by their Head, while the soldiers did the fighting. In the second coup, as the Head of Police flatly refused to co-operate or give in, it meant that no ministerial arrests could be made by the Police. The few troops available to Acheampong were more urgently needed on other assignments, than to be used for arresting ministers and party-officials.

The radio kept on repeating that all Ministers, Deputy Ministers, top party-officials were to report to the nearest Police

Station for their own arrest, or face the military consequences. The Police received no orders to effect any arrests, so none could be made. As a matter of fact, at about 10 am of 13 January, 1972, when I reported to my nearest Police Station (close to the Residence of the British High Commissioner in ACCRA) for my arrest, as required by the radio announcement, I was told by the duty officer that they had received no orders to effect any arrests and that I should go home free. He went further to inform me that the Minister of Trade and Tourism (almost the number three in the Cabinet) had also reported and had been told to go home. As such I went home, and began to organise the removal of my personal effects from the official residence to my private house in Accra.

Meanwhile, all over the country, it appeared that the coup was flopping, as no military units, apart from the initial ones, took part in it. The State Radio continued to play military music, interspersed every fifteen minutes with Acheampong's recorded announcement of the coup, the dissolution of the Busia Government, Parliament, the suspension of the 1969 Constitution, and the requirement that all ministers and top party officials were to report at the nearest Police Stations. Occasionally some classical music was thrown in to relieve the tedium of listening all the time to martial music!

While each military unit waited to see what the other would do, ultimately, the coup-makers consolidated their position by exploiting this psychological advantage. In effect, they met with no organised military opposition, although all those opposed to them did not like or approve of what they were doing. By late afternoon of 13 January, having previously announced the formation of a new military Government, the National Redemption Council (N.R.C.) – the conspirators announced the dismissal and detention of the Police Chief, Mr Bob Ampaw, and his replacement by his deputy, Mr J.H.Cobbina. The latter threw in his lot with the new régime and immediately ordered the nationwide arrests of all ministers, senior party officials and other prominent supporters of the overthrown Government. The Police now began their arrests in earnest.

I was in my private house in Accra, supervising the unloading of my belongings and those of my family, when a Police Jeep with four heavily-armed policemen came to take me away. It was about 5 pm on 13 January 1972. Having been driven to my official residence to collect a few personal toiletries and clothes, I said goodbye to my wife, my mother (who had driven 45 miles from our town, Agona Swedru, to Accra to see me, on hearing the radio announcements), and to my personal physician and family friend, a Yugoslav lady doctor Dr Djorjevic. As I left all three ladies in tears, I was whisked away to the very Police Station where I had earlier reported in the morning. This time there was a change.

There were also other senior ministers and the head of state security (Civil branch), Mr E.K.Mintah, still clutching in one hand the Bible, and the other his walkie-talkie, right to the very end. As a former House Prefect of mine, at Ghana's prestigious school, Achimota, I found the reunion and the circumstances most poignant. And I was not grieved in any way, when in the late evening, orders came through the Police wireless system that he should be released forthwith, as he was a civil servant. So my former Prefect gave me his best wishes, shook my hand and left for home, while I and my incoming political colleagues, awaited the Police vans to take us to prison to begin our long period of incarceration.

In all the major cities and towns in Ghana similar arrests were simultaneously taking place, with a few ministers slipping through the wide net. Some of the ministers, including J.H.Mensah (Finance), R.R.Amponsah, (Education) and others tried to journey to Kumasi, the capital of Ashanti, to organise

114

mass support and a Government-in-exile, but it was all too late. They were arrested on their mission. By the evening of the same fateful day, the neutral army units had all thrown in their lot with the new régime, thus consolidating its power and hold. By about 9 pm the conspirators, although still nervous and unsure of events yet to come, felt confident enough to appear on nation-wide radio and television to introduce themselves and their new Government.

Prominent in the new Government, with Acheampong himself as Chairman, were commanders of the two most powerful units in Accra, who had been in the conspiracy from its nebulous days to its hour of triumph. Thus the peasant boy from the village of Akruofum in Ashanti, with little education, social connections, but endowed with plenty of cunning, dishonesty and an immense capacity to beguile and deceive, had made it to the very top. Through a clever manipulation of his good gifts and evil talents, he was able to stay on top of the political ladder for a longer period in Ghana, than any other leader, except Dr Kwame Nkrumah. The success and failure of Ignatius Kutu Acheampong is a study in the venality of human nature, and offers palpable support of the old adage that indeed "honesty is the best policy", ultimately.

As soon as he was fully entrenched in power Col. Acheampong, or "The Chairman", as he preferred to be called, set out meticulously to undo all the salutary, but harsh economic measures which the Busia Government had been forced to take. To begin with, he was acclaimed as a hero by almost the whole nation. There were demonstrations throughout the nation, especially in the regional capitals. Market-women, students, Trade Unionists, civil servants, applauded Col. Acheampong for having come to deliver the country from the hands of the so-called "best-brains" of the nation. Prominent chiefs sent in powerful resolutions praising him, and welcoming his "timely intervention". All the aggrieved groups and parties which had, in one way or another, suffered the economic squeeze under Busia, felt so elated that they openly and publicly showed their ardent fervour, even when it was imprudent to do so. Well-known Lebanese businessmen were seen openly jubilating in white, because their adversary, the Busia régime, had been overthrown. Wives and relatives of the 568 civil servants who were dismissed in the 1970 Apollo exercise were too happy to express their joy. And the students, were happy that the Government of so-called intellectuals and pseudo-intellectuals had been toppled. In fact, watching some of the demonstrations, one would be justified to wonder whether those shouting and screaming against the overthrown Government, were the very people who had enthusiastically and excitedly welcomed the advent of that same Government to power on 1 October 1969, only a matter of 27 months ago. The people, completely oblivious of their immediate experiences of tyranny and dictatorship, shed no visible tears over the demise of the first post-coup, democratic, civilian administration in Ghana. Indeed, the demonstrators seemed to show a masochistic wish for the bad old days of repression and one-man rule.

These demonstrations by the public, plus the open support which the Civil Service, students, businessmen, traders and prominent intellectuals and opposition politicians gave Acheampong must have convinced him that he was indeed the "Redeemer of Ghana", as he and his new Government claimed to be. After all, the new Administration was called the National Redemption Council (N.R.C.). Street names and other similar landmarks became overnight translated from "National Liberation" streets or circles, or squares, to those of "Redemption".

Basking in this limitless public adulation, Col. I.K. Acheampong set out to redeem the country, according to his own ideas and fashion.

116

Politically, he strode the whole scene like a collossus who neither expected nor feared any challenge from any quarter. After ensuring the arrests of all the major supporters and followers of the previous régime, he set out, foresightedly, to build a political base for himself. Unlike the previous military régime, Acheampong made no definite committment to a return to civilian rule, except the vague, nebulous statements to the effect that there would be a return to civilian rule "when the economy was healthy", or "when the people are ready" or "when the country's economy was on its feet again". Anybody who was conversant with the state of Ghana economy knew that these statements, translated into realistic terms, meant the dim future – certainly not a matter of five or ten years. As Acheampong, right from the beginning, did not commit himself to a return of civilian rule, he felt free and justified often to state in public that he had come into office without the people's votes, and did not need them, and was going to put the country straight through the barrel of a gun, the same way he had catapulted himself into high office.

This was a constant refrain in his speeches, especially in the first few years of his administration. Nor could people complain. For having acquiesced in the overthrow of democracy, they could not, so immediately after the event, be also demanding the restoration of democracy.

Following the arrests of the ministers and other party officials, and feeling fully consolidated in power, Acheampong began to reward all his supporters and keep trouble at bay. First, he tackled the economy. Although claiming to be non-political, and neither left nor right, he started the sort of public rhetoric which clearly showed the intelligent observer that he was determined to bring back the economic set-up of the Nkrumah days. Such statements as "capturing the commanding heights of the economy" frequently peppered his public speeches. The problem was that as he himself had served as a Commissioner of the military régime after Nkrumah, and therefore, presumably approved the removal of Nkrumah, any pro-Nkrumah stand appeared rather illogical. Although not an intellectual, he was astute enough to know that although the people had hailed his overthrow of Busia, they wanted Nkrumah even less. To complicate Acheampong's problem, his three most powerful colleagues on the new military junta were all Ewes, from the Volta Region. And during the Nkrumah, apart from Ashanti, the Volta Region had been the main centre of opposition to Nkrumah's rule. As such, right from the beginning Acheampong's statements see-sawed between approving and disapproving the Nkrumah régime.

He appointed Kwame Karikari, an Ashanti, then Acting Head of the Economics Department at the Cape Coast University, as his Chief economic adviser. With Acheampong himself as Commissioner (i.e. Minister) of Finance, advised by Kwame Karikari, Acheampong set in motion his economic policy. First the Armed Forces. All the privileges and perks which had been removed by the Busia régime were immediately restored and improved. Acheampong then went one step further than the first military régime, when only a handful of senior officers had been seconded to the civil administration as Regional Commissioners, Ambassadors, General Managers and Managing Directors. In all, not more than twenty had been so deployed. Although they had sacrificed their lives to remove Nkrumah, they felt that even under a military régime, civilians should run the administration.

Acheampong was not going to make that mistake. He felt that with the gamble which he and his colleagues took they were entitled to the full fruits of their labours. He launched into a full-scale secondment of senior military officers into all the State Corporations, Ministries, and semi-state institutions. Officers were appointed in good numbers as Ambassadors, managing directors, managers, Commissioners (i.e. Ministers). In all the major aspects of public life, the soldiers, entered in full. Even junior officers and soldiers were given jobs in the general administration of the country. No section of the country's life was spared, as Acheampong men and loyal supporters from the Army were spread all over the country, to ensure that they got some of the civilian perks and comforts. The soldiers were indeed riding high, and any question of their returning to barracks became more and more academic.

The farmers were not forgotten. Local prices of cocoa and other produce were raised, and there were increased subsidies for fertilizers, chemicals, farm implements, fishing nets and fishing engines. Thus although the cost of living was still high, the farmers and fishermen had more money at their disposal to spend on the goods which were available. Nor did Acheampong forget the University students. He scrapped the loans-scheme which had been introduced by the Busia Government, and thus endeared himself to the students by a bold, though foolhardy economic measure.

Before its overthrow the Busia Government had gone into endless negotiations with the West about the country's enormous foreign debt. Busia quite rightly maintainted that as a democratic, civilian Government, which respects international law, it should accept these debts and negotiate with the West, especially Britain, to reschedule them, or have some of them cancelled, if possible, to help the Ghana economy. From 1970 to the demise of the régime, these negotiations had gone on endlessly, apparently yielding no positive results from Ghana's point of view. Indeed, the farcical situation had been reached when some members of the public were making cruel jokes about the Government, describing its members as "the spineless gentlemen who are always running to Britain with begging bowls and always returning home empty-handed". Busia's lack of success on the loans front was thus becoming a huge public joke, and a big political liability.

Soon after assuming office, in one of his earliest public statements, Acheampong arbitrarily and unilaterally, repudiated these debts by stating simply that his Government, unlike the previous one, "would act as men", and not pay the debts. Suddenly, this new policy on the debts, popularly known as "Yentua" (i.e. "we will not pay" in Akan) added to his national popularity. The press, radio, television all sang his praises, and the University students in Legon mounted huge demonstations before the British High Commission in Accra, not only against Britain, but as their show of solidarity for the "Yentua" policy. It appeared that overnight the soldier had succeeded where the statesman had failed.

Anticipating a stoppage of further commercial credits from the West, Acheampong announced that in future all Ghana's imports would be paid for spot-cash, without respite to the previous 180 day credit system, which had allowed the country to import its needs and pay for them later. Luckily for Acheampong his assumption of office coincided with a high level of prices on the world market for Ghana's chief exports – cocoa, timber, gold, diamonds, manganese and bauxite. Consequently, his new policy of cash payments for imports could be maintained for a while, until catastrophe set in.

The public servants were not forgotten either . All the rent and other increases which had been introduced by the Busia Government were removed; their allowance; were restored, and their conditions of service improved upon. The 568 civil servants who had been retired during the Busia régime were given the option of re-instatement in their jobs.

Although he did not write off completely the 44 per cent devaluation of the cedi which had been introduced by the Busia Government in late December 1971, the new régime re-valued the cedi reducing its devaluation from 44 to 25 per cent in February, 1972. By this action, the victorious and triumphant chairman of the N.R.C. was able to reduce the prices of imported goods and food items, to the happy satisfaction of Ghanaians.

The truth of the matter is that for the first few years of his rule (1972-74) Col. Acheampong benefitted tremendously from the economic infrastructure which had been laid by the Busia Administration. The Acheampong administration thus came to inherit a number of loan and other economic schemes from the West for which it had contributed nothing, and which it knew nothing about. The false picture of affluence and economic well-being which was thus evident in the first few years of the Acheampong régime can be traced to the remarkable success of Busia's administration in the field of Ghana-West relations. It had nothing to do with Acheampong's régime, although he claimed credit for it. On the contrary, his growing public statements and actions progressively ensured that, with the implementation and completion of the programmes and schemes already launched before his arrival on the scene, no further aid programmes would emanate from the same Western sources. To ensure that his public standing as a nationalist was even higher than that of his predecessor, in May 1972, Acheampong issued a decree whereby the State took the majority shares in all major foreign businesses and enterprises.

Acheampong thus swiftly established himself as a national hero, who had taken decisive action against foreign (mostly British) commercial and economic interests; as opposed to the more cautions and finely-tuned approach of the Busia administration. The generous expenditure of State funds and facilities to all the major, vociferous and influential sections of the Ghanaian community, helped to consolidate Acheampong's arbitrary capture of power. And, step by step, he turned himself from a usurper of political power into a benign father-figure of the nation. Extravagant praise and commendations poured on him by prominent chiefs, civil servants, senior army officers, journalists, businessmen, Trade Unionists etc., especially in the period 1972-75. They were due to the man's popularity, or at least, the massive influence which he had on the nation as a whole.

Acheampong understood the exercise of power and patronage perhaps better than his tutored, political opponents. As the State-system accounted for about 80 per cent of all the actively-employed population it meant that he who controlled the state apparatus could hold the whole nation to ransom for a considerable length of time. Even the cocoa farmers and other peasants, depended on the Government to purchase their produce. The monopoly which the State held in all important aspects of national life and existence was massive and all-pervading. It made dissent, economic development and progressive social reform impossible.

As Economics Minister, Acheampong had full control over the internal and external finances of the country and he fully exploited this office to the maximum. As Finance Minister he had direct control over the import programme of the country, through the import-licence system. Thus his friends and supporters were granted generous amounts of import licences so that they could bring in goods, especially scarce items, to sell and make huge profits. The Office of Business Promotion which had been set up under the Busia régime to help Ghanaians with loans and funds to buy foreign businesses, or set up on their own, was under Chairman Acheampong, so he found it easy, by granting heavy loans and financial assistance, to make friends and influence people.

To be fair to the poor devil, he was ingenious enough not to limit his largesse to only his political supporters, friends, relatives and mistresses. Even his political opponents, including former Cabinet and junior ministers in the régime he had overthrown, also benefitted from his expansive approval of the loans they requested. Indeed, the astuteness of the man knew no limits. I am reliably informed that when approving a huge loan for a former Cabinet Minister, who after his release from Acheampong's 20 month imprisonment wished to go into business, Acheampong is alleged to have joked: "Let's give him some to 'chop' so that when the day of reckoning comes, he too would have something to answer for!" ('Chop' is colloquial Ghanaian-English word used to mean to 'enjoy' or 'live on', with the hidden understanding behind the word being that the whole transaction is fraught with dishonesty, bribery and corruption.)

By the direction of the nation's funds, under his general control as Head of State, and more immediately as Finance Minister, Acheampong not only bought friends, but also effectively stifled any political opposition. It was a well-known fact, that after their periods of imprisonment by Acheampong, following the coup, many of the former Ministers, deputy ministers and prominent party officials and supporters directly or indirectly benefitted from the hands of Acheampong. His generous grant of loans, import licences, business contracts, special franchises, road contracts, all made their survival and existence possible. They knew this. And Acheampong himself knew this only too well.

Furthermore, as the Bank of Ghana (The Central Bank) is under the Ministry of Finance, it meant that Acheampong could direct the Bank which foreign exchange contracts it should approve, which foreign transactions should be given priority in payment, and which major import orders should be allocated foreign exchange as a matter of priority. The patronage and power which were inherent in the office of Commissioner of

Finance was limitless, and Acheampong more than any other Ghanaian Head of State exploited this centre of the nation's finance system to the full. Soon after Acheampong's coming to power, the Governor of the Bank and heads of the major finance institutions within the state system were removed and new men were appointed by the new régime.

While all this was going on, Acheampong articulately endeared himself to the people by frequently visiting different parts of the country, to fervent and excited public acclamation. Furthermore, while making personal grants to various friends and supporters of his, he devoted considerable portions of state funds towards the building of more schools, hospitals, clinics and roads. In a country where social and medical amenities were in dire scarcity, where there was a huge demand for more schools, colleges, scholarships, hospitals, clinics, water-supply, roads, cheap housing and subsidized transportation, Acheampong's ability to provide these for a long while, made him popular to the extent that many people forgot the political, unconstitutional and indeed illegal antecedents of his régime. So long as Acheampong delivered the required goods, it was irrelevant to most people what he called his Government. Neither were they interested whether it was Left or Right, capitalist or socialist. When people are hungry and poor, such abstruse arguments are purely academic and of little relevance, if any, to their immediate, mundane problems. And right up to about 1976 it could be said that indeed Ignatius Kutu Acheampong was in the position to deliver the goods. This advantageous position of his was possible because prices for exports were favourable, whereas imports were controlled and their prices borne by the country's economy.

Eventually, even chairman Acheampong had to do his arithmetic. Like Nkrumah, he had to pay for the huge socialist fare of vast public expenditure which he had been giving the people to keep them quiet. The progressive world economic crisis, especially from 1975, the fall in export earnings and the rise in import bills were to force Acheampong to cut down on public expenditure, limit imports and re-introduce some of the severe cuts of the Busia régime. Thus the civil servants' rent which had been reduced from Busia's 20 per cent to 10 per cent in 1973, was now raised to 15 per cent. Some other allowances to public servants were minimised, but not removed altogether. The policy of heavy subsidies for imported food items, e.g. milk, sugar, corned beef, sardines, kerosine lamps, fuel, was reviewed and considerably reduced. The nett result of these new measures was to cause a tremendous increase in the cost of living. The basic staples mentioned above became scarce and very exhorbitant in prices. The economic situation was getting more and more desperate. As people compared their economic position then with what it had been under the Busia régime, they could not but conclude that at least under Busia, the goods and food were available, even thought their prices were high. Now the goods and food items were *not* available.

Acheampong and his men tried to blame all this on the world crisis, the world inflation, the jump in oil-prices. But alas, such arguments and pleas no longer fell on receptive ears. Acheampong had promised to "redeem" them from their sufferings under Busia, and now, as they saw it, the "redemption" had made their lot worse! By December 1976, the standard of living of the Ghanaian was at the lowest ebb in the history of the country. As food shortages mounted, queues for food and other essential commodities grew larger and more desperate. Acheampong let loose the soldiers on the people. And the soldiers began to beat mercilessly men and women, especially the latter, for allegedly forming queues to embarras and disgrace the Government. This was a far cry from the days of early 1972 when the same people were jubilating over the fall of the Busia Government and the arrival of Col. Acheampong and his men on the political scene!

By 1977 Acheampong was facing an immense politico-economic dilemma. For the first time since capturing office, the master-conjurer was at his wits' end. He looked into the crystal-ball and what he saw was most distressing. However grave the economic situation became, which grew progressively worse, month by month, there were two major actions which chairman Acheampong refused to take, even at the peril of his life. First, as the Commissioner or Minister of Defence, he was responsible for the Armed Forces upon whom he absolutely depended. This dependence became more significant as the economy of the country got worse. For him to cut down on the privileges, perks, service conditions of the Armed Forces would have spelt an immediate doom to his own survival. As the instinct for survival is fundamental to every human-being, a shrewd pragmatic, machiavellian politician like Acheampong had no difficulty in seeing that the last thing to do was to interfere with the privileges and service conditions of the military forces. Acheampong would not under any circumstances annoy the Army, and thus give them an excuse to do to him, in late 1976-77, what he had done, with their help, to the Busia régime in January 1972. He might be ignorant and simple, but certainly not a fool!

Secondly, his survival instincts further told him that as soon as he devalued the cedi, as the local and international experts (including the I.M.F., and other reputable, international bodies) were advising him to do for the best interests of the national economy, the bells would probably be tolled for his political and indeed physical funeral. One of the major reasons he had given for his sudden, unwarranted and unjustified military intervention in January 1972 to destroy a freely-elected, civilian, democratic Government was the December 1971 devaluation of the cedi by

126

that Government. Now here he was being invited by his local and foreign advisers and experts to literally preside over the liquidation of his empire, and his own personal demise. Acheampong flatly refused to commit suicide.

At least on two occasions details of a possible devaluation were worked out and a date fixed for the official announcement. At the last minute, Acheampong, on second thought, refrained from taking the major step towards the urgently-needed resuscitation of the economy.

Instead of adopting the remedies being canvassed on him by economic experts, who saw those measures as the only way left to him, Acheampong dreamed out ingenious cunning schemes of his own. With prices rocketing and with everybody grumbling, something had to be done to redeem the situation. He set out to do precisely that. To re-vamp his administration, he sacked his Chief Economic Adviser, Kwame Karikari, who had since the early days of the coup been his right-hand man and virtual "Finance Minister". He was appointed to the far less powerful job of Head of the Special Action Unit.*

Although, he later appointed first a military officer, then a civilian economist, and finally a military officer, as his "special assistant to the Commissioner of Finance", the fact still remains that Acheampong was fully in control of the nation's finance till the last day.

As aid and loans from Western Governments and other reputable finance houses had virtually dried up by 1976-77, Acheampong took to borrowing on the free world money market. Subsequently, a Commission of Enquiry in 1978 into these loans and financial arrangements was to report most adversely on some of them. The grand scale of bribery and corruption which had all along been suspected to be going on with these loans were fully confirmed and exposed. The Amissah Committee's Report on Government loans published in

1979 showed the extent to which some prominent Ghanaian citizens, including the Redeemer himself, had conspired to dupe the country of its very precious foreign exchange then available. The more Acheampong's régime borrowed, the worse the deficit in its balance of payment became and the lower the value of the cedi fell. Although by 1977 Acheampong still refused to devalue the cedi officially, the currency had been unofficially devalued.

Instead of its official rate of exchange of one cedi to the U.S. dollar, it was being charged at *ten* cedis to the dollar on the black market, to the knowledge of many people who cared to know, including some military officers.

By the system of Special Unnumbered Licence, (S.U.L.) a person or firm could bring in goods without import licence, if it did not ask for foreign exchange transfer to pay for the goods abroad. The individual concerned, having charged his cedis to dollars at 10:1, instead of 1:1, the official rate, would then sell the goods at prices that ensured about 100 per cent profit or more. Obtaining more cedis, these would be then changed back into dollars or pounds sterling and the whole exercise repeated. The S.U.L. system had been introduced with the Foreign Exchange Controls in 1961 to help bring in more goods as the country's foreign exchange was very limited. There were genuine cases of people or firms with money abroad who wanted to bring in more goods to help the state. Unfortunately, over a period of years it had become progressively abused to constitute the hotbed of the black-market in Ghana.

Previous administrations had toyed with the idea of abolishing it completely, but this was never done. Under Acheampong it was briefly suspended in 1977, but then allowed to feely thrive and flourish a few months later. The Commissioner of Trade and Tourism under Acheampong, an upright accountant-soldier, who had as a sideline become an Anglican priest, advocated the abolishing of the S.U.L. system, rightly blaming it for Ghana's inflation rate in 1977-78 of about 150 per cent. Right till the demise of his Government he was not listened to. Indeed he was sent to Coventry by some of his colleagues in the Government and Army for making a nuisance of himself! When the day of reckoning did come, his earlier protestations and honest stand did not help him much. He was badly and mercilessly beaten and physically assaulted in a very inhumane manner. The S.U.L. system was eventually abolished in July 1978, with the catastrophic, though inevitable, fall of Acheampong.

Apart from borrowing heavily from unofficial sources outside, in order to put more money into circulation, the régime ordered the printing of more paper money, especially from 1978. Thus with few goods and food items about, but plenty of cash, the galloping inflation got out of control completely. Suddenly a few people became "cedi-millionaires" and a standard loaf of bread was costing about five cedis, i.e. £2.50 (or $5.0) at the official rate of exchange. A tin of milk was then about 4 cedis, i.e. about £2 or $4. The gravity of the situation of the ordinary man can be gauged when it is remembered that the average monthly wage was about 69 cedis, or less.

Such an abnormal economic situation thus multiplied many times the endemic bribery and corruption which had been in existence before Independence and after. One major side-effect of the economic policies of the Acheampong administration was to raise the level of bribery and corruption in the nation to unbelievably high levels. With cost of living and prices so unreasonably high, it was naive not to expect people at all levels of human endeavour to find ways and means of supplementing their wages or incomes. Bribery, corruption, forgery, immoral living, larceny, all became a way of life, and for good reasons too. The very existence of many people and their families was at stake.

The increased manifestations of these evil, anti-social habits were not limited to the ordinary people. With the progressive introduction of more and more officers and soldiers into the general running of the country following the coup, it became increasingly clear to many people that the officers and soldiers, in their fight against bribery and corruption, had become afflicted with the same social diseases that civilians suffered from, namely graft, corruption, greed, avarice, nepotism. Although subsequent commissions of enquiry were to confirm these public fears and suspicions, long before these reports, the intelligent public knew that they were going on. There were no other rational explanations for the sudden wealth, in cash, luxurious cars and residential property, which had suddenly come the way of officers and men who, before the coup, had very little and lived in modest circumstances in the barracks. The sudden change in life-style of themselves and their wives, relatives and friends was a positive indication of what was going on. What made the whole despicable situation intolerable was that such corruption and fraud was being perpetrated by people who had overthrown a freely-elected, democratic, civilian Government on charges of corruption.

To buttress his tottering régime and salvage his falling popularity, Acheampong, from about December 1976, began to take a more active and direct part in the allocation and direction of the import licence programme. A special import licence allocation, to be used at his own discretion, was made to him by his Government. Out of this huge vote he dispensed licences for specific goods to friends and people who approached or appealed to him. Many young men and women, especially the latter, suddenly sprang into existence as businessmen and women. They flourished and made considerable fortunes. Prominent among the recipients of his generosity were many old politicians from both the Nkrumah and Busia régimes retired, or dismissed Army officers, friends, relatives and any who had the opportunity of being introduced to him.

As foreign exchange available to the nation became more and more limited, especially from 1975, Acheampong took a more personal interest in the way the Bank of Ghana made foreign exchange available for payments of certain imports or commitments.

After a series of long committee meetings the Bank of Ghana and the Ministries of Finance and Trade had worked out careful allocations for the nation's imports. However, the Head of State directly, some times by telephone to the Governor, or some times through the Cabinet Secretary or the special Assistant for Finance got all these well-thought out plans dislocated by asking for direct and immediate payments to be made for particular imports, contracts or agreements. Thus funds which had been set aside for importing, medicines, spare parts, books or other items, had to be diverted to meet the Chairman's wishes. And when the Deputy Governor of the Bank, Mr Annoh, responsible for overseas payments, tried to show the Head of State that certain payments he wanted could not be made, he was publicly dismissed.

A similar fate befell his superior officer, Dr S. Amon-Nikoi, a mild, honest Achimota-educated, Harvard-trained economist. He refused to make certain payments for armoured cars which the Head of State had unilaterally negotiated with a Swiss-based firm. The requested payments would have meant diverting urgently needed funds from essential supplies.

While attending a major international conference of bankers and financiers, in London, Dr Nikoi, without being previously informed, was dismissed by an announcement on the national radio.

But this policy of manipulating the foreign exchange programme through unwarranted interference with the Bank of Ghana, by direct verbal or telephone orders, or through written orders by Chairman Acheampong in his famous green-ink missives could not change the fundamental economic problems of Ghana. This was the acute insufficiency of foreign exchange to pay for the urgently-needed imports of the country. The situation had become so desperate that by 1977 basic items such as toothpaste, toothbrush, toilet paper, soap, milk, corned beef and sardines were simply not available. The scarce few that could be seen went only to a few selected families, while the rest of the population had to spend hours struggling to get them, even at the inflated prices.

Acheampong's dilemma was acute, considering that he had treacherously overthrown the civilian Government because the prices of basic consumer goods and food were too high, and that the Government was corrupt. By 1977, prices were astronomical. And corruption among his redeeming officers in the civil administration was well-known to the public.

Acheampong's capacity for scheming and inventiveness was limitless. Acting on the advice of his various confidents, who constituted a sort of "kitchen Cabinet" (journalists, frustrated politicians, disappointed academics, etc.) Acheampong tried to check the rapid down-drift towards economic collapse. A hotch-potch of distribution systems were tried.

Thus the Government became directly responsible for the distribution of the essential items which were in short supply. This did not work. The Government tried to appoint special local distributors. This did not work. The Government tried to appoint special local distributors. This did not work either. It tried to do a deal on very unorthodox lines, (and contrary to regulations) over the head of the Bank of Ghana, with certain Western firms to supply certain items at special prices, particularly favourable to the suppliers.

The latter action brought only a temporary relief to the nation's economic headaches. There appeared simply to be no end to the economic misfortunes plaguing the régime. And while the economic situation became worse and worse and more intractable, the political situation was catapulting into a state of anarchy, which even the Redeemer himself was helpless to deal with.

---

* This was a civilian department based in the Castle, employing soldiers supposedly to ferret out economic crimes and sabotage, and smooth the implementation of Government policies and decrees. Later on, it was to degenerate into a vicious, secret, strong-arm feature of the Government, harrassing everyone suspected of so-called economic or political sabotage and wrong-doing.

Chapter 8 – Destined to Die

Even though Acheampong had been welcomed and hailed as a national hero by practically the whole country, with the continuing deterioration of the nation's economy, especially from 1977, his popularity began to wane tremendously. Thus, from being a popular man that could go anywhere, anytime, in the early years of his rule, he had become a leader who could not go anywhere, at any time. As his unpopularity became more and more evident, Acheampong set out cunningly to save first his régime, and, failing that, his own life at the expense of his comrades-in-arms.

He came to rely more and more on the Military Intelligence in the Army and the Special Banch of the Police Force. Ruthlessly, he exploited these two organisations to ferret out and harrass genuine and imaginary political opponents. Arbitrary arrests and searches without warrants became more and more common, and the least whiff of dissent or opposition was snuffed out by the Special Branch and the Military Intelligence. Many of those arrested were mercilessly beaten, interrogated and detained (i.e. imprisoned without trial for long periods). The lucky ones were only beaten, and released after a few weeks imprisonment. The Director of Millitary Intelligence at the time allegedly claimed that while he continued as D.M.I. there would be no coup. Indeed, how right he was.

By heavily patronising the Military Intelligence and the Special Branch, Acheampong succeeded completely in stifling all growing opposition to his régime. Several attempted coups were aborted by the security services. Prominent among these attempts were those in 1972 involving a group of dedicated, patriotic intellectuals at the Ghana University. Centred around the former Head of Special Branch, Mr Ofosu-Armaah, who, after his release from prison at the time of the coup, had resumed his former position as Senior Lecturer in Law at the University, this was a bold and well-planned attempt to restore constitutional law in Ghana. Unfortunately, the efficiency of the security services led to the collapse of this noble effort. In 1973 a similar fate befell another prominent politician and ex-trade unionist Alex Hamah. His efforts to organise a counter-coup to effect the release of the imprisoned former Government ministers and top party officials and restore constitutional government also failed. In both these attempts and others, the "coup-makers" had been egged on by a well-known favourite of Acheampong, Col. Bob Kotei, who had won rapid promotion, under Acheampong, and had become, in turn, commander of the First Infantry Brigade, and later Army Commander.

That all these bold and well-planned attempts to dislodge Acheampong failed, is partly explained by the overall efficiency and pervading nature of the activities of the security services, and also the tremendous hold which Acheampong had over the Armed Forces generally.

Acheampong had three major advantages which the two previous leaders, Nkrumah and Busia, did not enjoy. First, unlike them, he was a soldier and not a civilian, and thus was seen by the soldiers as one of them, even though circumstances had catapulted him into the highest office in the land. Second, even as Head of State, Acheampong continued to identify himself with the Armed Forces, especially the ordinary ranks. For he himself had joined the Army as a private and risen through the ranks to become a Lt. Colonel by 1971. He widely maintained his old contacts within the Army, who often had direct access to him either in his office at the Castle, or in the military headquarters at Burma Camp. He could thus by-pass their senior officers and deal directly with the troops through his old contacts and friends. Third, having exploited treachery and his military position to capture the Government, he had naturally developed a keen nose for smelling out potential treachery "wherever it might emanate from", but especially from the Army. Consequently while lavishing generous service conditions on the Armed Forces, strengthening the Military Intelligence and Special Branch, and fully exploiting his old military contacts, both senior and junior, Acheampong resorted to frequent changes in command in the Armed Forces on the least doubts or suspicions of disloyalty.

Soon after assuming office, a number of senior officers were either appointed ambassadors, given other civilian jobs or "retired" from the Army. By the latter process, Brigadier Asare, who had been jumped over as First Infantry Brigade Commander in late 1971 by the Busia Government, to the advantage of Acheampong, was appointed Army Commander and soon "retired" from the Army. Other colleagues and contemporaries of his, were also gradually eased out of the Army.

Furthermore, Acheampong developed into a fine art the old and flawless principle of government, *imperio et divisio* – divide and rule. For a long time, he realised that by carefully manipulating one senior officer against the other, he could effectively keep them at loggerheads for as long as possible, thus obviating any possibility of their coming together to plan a coup or revolt against him. For as long as his opponents or potential enemies were busy suspecting and undermining each other, they would naturally have little time, thought or heart for scheming collectively against him.

Following the retirement in 1975 of the then Chief of Defence Staff (C.D.S.), Ashley-Larsen, previously Commander of the Air Force, Acheampong appointed the current Head of the Air

Force, Brigadier Charles Beausoleil, a brilliant and experienced pilot and staff officer as Acting C.D.S. It was assumed by many intelligent observers that with his experience, talent and flair, Beausoleil, would eventually be confirmed as C.D.S. Acheampong, however, had other ideas. He appointed as Commissioner for N.R.C. Affairs, the former Defence Adviser (i.e. Military Attaché) of Ghana in Washington, Col. Okai, who became virtually head of the security services. Both Okai and Beausoleil, were contemporaries at Ghana's prestigious school, Achimota, and had had similar military backgrounds – one in the air-force, the other in the army. Both were possible contenders for the enviable position of C.D.S. After keeping the two men in suspense and divided, with inspired rumours attributed against each other, Acheampong eventually gave the post to Okai, although his rival was the more senior professionally. Beausoleil thus reverted to his former position as Head of the Air Force. Continuously trying to keep the two men as far apart and as distrusting of each other as possible, Acheampong eventually, in 1977, gave a technical knock-out to both of them simultaneously. His régime accused both men of corruption and evasion of customs-duties on their imported cars and mounted a vigorous, public campaign on the radio, television and press against them as dangerous enemies of State, and as so-called "C.I.A. Agents". With the State controlling and owning the mass media, there was simply no way of these publicly accused and disgraced officers putting forward their case. Both were quickly promoted and "retired" from the service, after the Government had announced amounts and indemnities to the Customs and Excise which they were to pay.

The removal of these two men led to further changes in the Command structure, with General Akuffo, a brilliant parachute officer of impeccable record, climbing from the post of Army Commander to Chief of Defence Staff. His old position was taken by Bob Kotei, an old friend and favourite of Acheampong.

For the first time the disgrace and removal of the two senior officers in 1977 was beginning to fill some of Acheampong's staunchest supporters in the Army, and in Military Intelligence, with considerable unease. Being intelligent, observant people, they were now at last beginning to discern Acheampong's clever game of "divide and rule". They belatedly began to see that what had happened to others could easily happen to them. And the more foresighted ones among them began to reflect on the whole future of the Armed Forces and their own future too. The less gifted among them still felt that they would be excluded or exempt from Acheampong's insidious attack on the Army. They were naive enough to think that others might go, but that they would stay. They had apparently forgotten the popular Akan proverb which says "se wodze Kojo a na wodze wo." [Freely translated it means "if Kojo is being held today, then know that you would be held tomorrow."]

Acheampong's cunning and scheming knew no end. The brilliance of this move against his two most senior and most powerful officers (apart from his protegé, the Army Commander, Bob Kotei) can be fully understood when it is remembered that he had only in the previous year used these same two men and others, to dislodge all his chief lieutenants and former comrades-in-arms on the National Redemption Council, N.R.C.

From the day of his successful capture of power on, it had become popular knowledge that the most powerful and influential members of the new military régime were Major Selormey, head of the Recce Regiment, Major Agbo, and Major Kwame Baah. These were the three officers who had been in on the conspiracy from the very beginning, and whose troops had made the whole exercise a success. Being in the south, they were all under Acheampong, as Brigade Commander.

139

Acheampong's success was thus a joint effort. As such, although junior in rank to their senior officers and commanders in the barracks, by the very reason that they were on the military junta ruling the country, including the armed forces, they had far more power, authority and influence than their military commanders. The odd and ridiculous situation thus arose whereby these so-called "coup-makers", or "coup-boys", were superior in office and in the state hierarchy to persons to whom they were inferior to in rank and position in the Army itself. Acute problems of command and discipline were inevitable!

The three joint coup-makers with Acheampong, feeling their own strength, were publicly-known to have, on a number of occasions, challenged Acheampong or take him to task in a way and manner that not even his most senior colleagues dared contemplate. As all of them continued to live in the same compound as before the coup, Acheampong could not cut himself off from their direct personal onslaughts, if even he had wished to do so. If before the coup, they could visit him freely and talk frankly to him as Brigade Commander, why could they not do it now, after they had put him where he now was? To them, as *Chairman*, he was merely *primus inter pares*. Indeed, the original idea to rotate the chairmanship had been mooted, but quickly abandoned, as being unworkable. Acheampong's control over his three colleagues was thus only nominal, and was patently irksome.

Seizing on these personal difficulties with the "coup-boys", and the frequent complaints by the Senior service commanders about the breakdown in discipline, which was resulting from the highly anomalous position of senior commanders and officers having to take orders from their junior colleagues on the Military junta, Acheamopng in September 1976 demoted the National Redemption Council (N.R.C.) as the ruling body of the nation, and superimposed on it a new Supreme Military Council (S.M.C.) which consisted of himself as Chairman, the Heads of

140

the Army, Navy, Air Force, the Head of the Police Force and the Head of the Border-Guards. His illustrious, but troublesome right-hand men from the coup days (Selormey, Agbo, Kwame Baah) were not appointed on the new military junta. They too refused to serve on the old N.R.C., which had now become castrated and demoted in authority. They were quickly and abruptly "retired" from the Army of Acheampong.

Simultaneously, the Head of State, who had by now accepted the promotion from Colonel to General, announced the creation of an Executive Council, to be made up of military officers holding civilian jobs, and the replacement of a number of military officers on the council, by civilians.

This move was made chiefly to revamp the blackening image of the régime, to bring in new blood, and to assuage public demands for a greater participation of civilians in the country's administration. It is true that the Acheampong régime, unlike the previous military régime (1966-69) had not committed itself to a return to civilian rule. Indeed, Acheampong boastfully stated, in the heyday of his rule, that he had come to power by the barrel of the gun and intended to rule likewise. His determination and intention to rule civilians without civilian approval or support was made quite clear from the beginning. There was not going to be any nonsense about democracy, civilian rule, return to barracks, and all that. Of course, the dim hope was sometimes held before the country, of a possible limited return to civilian rule, but it was never made definite.

But even Acheampong, with all his deviousness and ruthlessness, could not stop the march of history. As his régime progressed, and became more and more dictatorial, the public interest in a return to democratic, civilian rule grew more and more persistent and louder. And it was in a partial answer to these public clamours and requests that he had brought in a number of prominent civilians into the administration as

Commissioners. The power still lay with the S.M.C., especially with Acheampong, as Chairman. For as the new body, devoid of the "coup-boys", did not include any man or officer of substance, who had jointly executed the coup in January 1972 with Acheampong, it meant that effectively the new S.M.C. members were beholden to Acheampong for their positions.

As they were all active service commanders, it meant that they had to divide their time and attention between their state duties on the junta and the military duties in the barracks. Acheampong, on the other hand, had the advantage of not holding any active state office, apart from that of Commissioner of Defence, and that of (nominal) Commissioner of Finance. He thus had more time and freedom to concentrate on his job as Head of State, supervising especially the survival of his own régime and his own life. He, therefore, had more time for ruling the country, than could be afforded by his other colleagues on the S.M.C. It was clear that the appointment of the Heads of the Army, Navy, Air Force, Border Guards, and Police on the S.M.C. was to leave them less and less time for S.M.C. affairs. Thus more and more power came to concentrate in the hands of the man who had the time and the interest to wield it.

Also by not officially appointing a deputy or vice-chairman, who would act for him, whenever possible and necessary, the chairman ensured that the rivalry, bickering and jostling for influence among the members of the new military junta, were actively kept alive, to his obvious advantage. The "coup-boys", except Kwame Baah, were both Ewes, who, like the Ashantis, had suffered very badly under the tyrannical period of Nkrumah. As such, so long as they were on the military junta they had a moderating influence on the pro-Nkrumah propensities of Acheampong. Thus in the first few years of the régime, before Acheampong consolidated his position in the military and in the nation, the farcical situation was evident whereby official statements tending to be pro-Nkrumah and against the coup of 1966, would be swiftly followed in a few days time by equally anti-Nkrumah statements, acquiescing in and hailing the coup of 1966, whose leader had been an Ewe (Kotoka) from the Volta Region.

Now, without the restricting influence of his three obstreperous young colleagues, Acheampong felt free to be himself. He began to talk with a tone and accent very reminiscent of Nkrumah. He took to wearing a "Mao-style" tunic and carry a flamboyant walking-stick like Nkrumah. He was sounding more and more left-ish in public and becoming more and more capitalist in private. For the vague details of his business and financial interests and those of his friends, relatives and colleagues were becoming publicly rumoured, day by day. It was then that a fact that had been glossed over all the time became public knowledge – that Acheampong had in the sixties attended the marxist, ideological institute at Winneba, while in the Army. The jigsaw puzzle was now becoming rather clearer and easier to disentangle, but by then it was too late. Acheampong was too firmly entrenched in power for it to be a safe and worthwhile proposition to bring these and other facts out about General Acheampong's social and political background.

With the progressive and rapid deterioration in the economy, and therefore his national image and prestige, Acheampong made a ruthless and desperate use of the mass-media, especially the Press. They were used to stifle dissent and opposition, indulge in character-assasination of suspected opponents or rivals, and for the exposition and disgrace of so-called spies and agents of the West, imperialism, C.I.A., colonialism.

In an obviously-orchestrated series of press attacks, the public was encouraged to think that all the economic woes and troubles, were due to greedy, frustrated ex-politicians, women-traders, decadent intellectuals and incorrigible boot-lickers of the West. But, by 1978, these statements had become stale and jarring on the ears of a hungry, disappointed and despondent public who now looked on nostalgically to the good old days of freedom and plenty of the Busia régime which Acheampong had replaced. Also the growing corruption among the officers in civilian jobs and of some of their colleagues back in the barracks, who were Acheampong's favourites, was becoming public knowledge, even if mutely expressed.

The Chairman's reaction to all these economic, political and other problems was to be more and more dictatorial. All sorts of decrees were issued against rumour-mongering, public meetings, associations, commerce and trade, and movement. Acheampong was obviously beginning to panic. While in the early days of his rule, wherever he went and waved his traditional white handkerchief, there had been massive ovation and cheers, by December 1977 he went about heavily escorted by a fleet of cars carrying armed men of the security services. Response to his waving of the white handkerchief was nil and sad. His daily route to the Castle had to be changed frequently and suddenly by the security services in order to defeat any possible attempts on his life. And it was even rumoured that he was not sleeping at his official residence, but at different places, haphazardly, to avoid kidnapping or assassination. Acheampong began to feel more and more isolated by 1977, and was indeed living a life of hell-on-earth, despite his official position as Head of State. He was secretly known to be suffering from insomnia, nervous exhaustion and general debility. His dependence on drink and drugs grew steadily with his worsening state, but to the last day, one major interest which he never relinquished was his excessive womanising. Indeed, a few hours before his last day when facing a nation-wide radio press and television audience in Accra in June 1979, on being questioned about his womanising as Head of State was bold and honest about it. He did not deny it and showed no remorse whatsoever.

As Acheampong became progressively desperate and isolated, he sought refuge in the occult and spiritualism and "juju" (voodooism), although nominally remaining a Roman Catholic. Indian gurus were flown in at State expense to be housed in State House to give spiritual direction and advice to the Head of State. Local and foreign spiritualists, reputedly powerful enough to avert harm and danger to the Head of State, were all consulted, at very high fees, readily paid in either local or foreign exchange. The numbers and activities of spies in all major aspects of the nation's life were increased, all to no avail. For the rapid progression towards the day of reckoning could not be avoided, even by the self-styled Redeemer, who had used treachery to achieve his ambitions. The moment of truth ws soon approaching for General Ignatius Kutu Acheampong.

As in 1972, the first major, organised groups to demonstrate in reaction to the situation in the country, was the university student body, but this time in May 1977, they were demonstrating not *for* Acheampong, as their predecessors had done, but *against* him. Superbly organised demonstrations took place in Accra, Kumasi and Cape Coast by the university students, not only against the mounting economic difficulties, high cost of living, but also against bribery and corruption in the Armed Forces, especially among those who had been seconded into civilian jobs. Furthermore, the demonstrations were against Acheampong's efforts to perpetuate his military rule indefinitely.

Achempong's régime, like the first military régime, had been haunted with the possibility of being replaced by a civilian Government which was unfriendly to it, and thus might institute criminal proceedings against the members of the military régime. To effect the political destruction of his political opponents, Acheampong had, on coming into office, set up two

Commissions of Enquiry, to investigate the assets, properties etc. of the Ministers, Deputy Ministers and other top officials of the overthrown party. Each person, while in prison, in January 1972, had been given a comprehensive questionnaire to fill giving details such as name, birth, education, career, salaries and allowances, from first year of working, right up to the day of the coup. Their wives were also required to fill in similar forms. Each person had to be probed or investigated before the Assets Committee to explain the sources of his or her assets and those of their children. Before the full glare of television, radio and the local press, these interrogations went on, after each person's questionnaire had been checked and rechecked by the Police and Special Branch.

The net result of this public interrogation was generally to humiliate these ex-Ministers and their wives and children. Admittedly, in the process, corruption on a very minor scale was unearthed among some of the former Ministers and top party officials. In such cases, the assets which were considered by the investigating committees to have been wrongfully or illegally acquired were confiscated to the State and their owners banned from holding public office for the rest of their lives.

Although by 1974, Acheampong had all these reports and the accompanying White Papers, he did not authorise their publication, holding them as a Damoclean sword over the heads of the disgraced persons concerned. A report involving the former Prime Minister, Dr K.A. Busia and other three Ministers was published in early 1977, at the height of the public grumblings and demonstrations, against the economic hardships. Although it concluded that some of the Ministers had assets and properties over and beyond their legitimate source of income, Dr Busia, however, could not appear personally before the investigating committee as required by the decree, so the Committee's conclusions on him can be challenged.

Having through detentions and public investigations and humiliations destroyed politically the members of the Government which he had overthrown, Acheampong was, despite his claims to the contrary, forced progressively to rely on the members and supporters of the civilian régime before that of Busia, namely the Nkrumah men. As such, although Acheampong often repeated that his coup was not meant for either the C.P.P. or P.P., he had little choice as he could not really appoint as Commissioners the very people he had just kicked out of office. He also came to rely more and more on politicians who had failed in the 1969 General Elections, who could be said to be against Busia and his party. By the very employment of these same rejected politicians, Acheampong caused a lot of harm. His attempts to solve his political problems by relying on some of the discredited politicians only tended to accentuate the intensity of the problems.

Meanwhile, unable to quell the student demonstrations and disturbances, despite the use of many undercover agents in the universities, Acheampong's régime let loose the Army and Police. In direct confrontations, a number of unarmed students participating in peaceful, legitimate demonstrations were shot at. At least eight were killed, and many more injured. As the demonstrations spread, the Universities were shut down indefinitely. Subsequently, Acheampong himself went on television to tell the whole nation that the Universities would remain closed, that he would not give in to their demands, and that the students receiving education he never had would be the losers, not he, as long as the institutions remained closed. With the highest institutions of learning shut down, with no hope of their immediate re-opening, some of the secondary schools also went on strike and were also shut down. The whole country was by early 1978, crippled with frustration, chaos and confusion, as students and pupils returned home to stay.

The political picture nationwide was dismal and could not have inspired Acheamong very much. Short of repeating the need for sacrifice by everyone, and the expressions of hope for a better future, there was very little he could effectively do. There was, of course, repression and brute force. And he resorted to these more and more as the situation became more and more intractable and hopeless. But what Acheampong appeared to forget was that, although he had ensured the Army's loyalty by acceeding to their requests for improved conditions of service, *it was impossible to isolate the Army from the civilian population whose economic sufferings were well known to the soldiers.* He also appeared to have forgotten that the same Military Intelligence, Special Branch, and other security people he relied on to prop his dictatorial régime, were derived from the very civilian population, whom he was again and again ordering them to harrass, terrorize or beat up. It needed little common sense to realise that very shortly the point was going to be reached when the very people propping the régime (or at least many of them) would begin to question the purpose of the whole exercise. Acheampong soon realised that, but it was almost too late!

The Army, on the whole, remained loyal to the very end, but the grumblings inside it went apace with those among the civilian population. Some officers had the courage of their convictions. Early in 1977 General Albert Ocran, whose intervention in the 1966 coup as brigade commander of the south, had assured the coup's success, made a bold challenge to the Acheampong régime. He wrote a long, learned petition to the régime in which he drew their attention to the rampant and well-known instances of bribery and corruption, greedy acquisition of wealth, abuse of office among officers in the barracks, particularly those who had been seconded to civilian positions. After giving details of his charges, General Ocran had gone further to expose the incongruity and lies behind the whole concept of *"Union Government"* which had been put forth by the régime. He boldly asked for a return to barracks by the Army, and the urgent need for the civilian people being allowed freely to choose their own civilian government immediately. The régime's retort to Ocran's reasoned petition was to put him under strict security surveillance, harrass him and his close friends, and ban him from all military establishments on pain of immediate arrest. But all this did not worry or surprise Ocran unduly.

A highly-principled man, he had become a member of the triumverate, the Presidential Commission, which was set up in October 1969, when the civilian administration of Busia took office. It consisted of Afrifa, as Chairman, J.W.K. Harlley, the Head of Police, and General A. Ocran. Following disagreements in the Commission, it had been dissolved and a new civilian President chosen in 1970. He was the former Chief-Justice, Justice Akuffo Addo, one of the three Supreme Court Judges who had been dismissed by President Nkrumah in 1963.

With the installation of the civilian President to replace the Presidential Commission, Afrifa had gone into business. Harlley went into farming. Ocran went to Oxford University to read law. His success at Oxford and his return were personally self-satisfying achievements. More so, they demonstrated to his army colleagues that at least some of them could successfully make the adjustment into civilian life with ease and promise. On his return to Ghana, Ocran concentrated on writing on military subjects and published two books in England. He was concerned enough about events in Ghana to have publicly reminded the Busia régime on the need for all of its members to declare their assets as required by the 1969 Constitution.

He also emphasized the urgency for the new civilian régime to abide by the spirit and letter of the Constitution. Undeterred by public comments attacking his point of view in 1971, Ocran

149

displayed the same zeal and dedication to public duty and the cause of truth, in 1977, as he had done in 1971, and in 1966. The measure of the man's honesty and moral and physical courage can be gauged by the fact that among those officers whose corruption and arbitrary rule he condemned and challenged in his celebrated petition to the military régime, was his own son-in-law, Acheampong protégé, Bob Kotei, who was then the Army Commander. In this bitter family quarrel involving affairs of State, General Ocran's wife, Nancy, no less celebrated a fighter for liberty and human rights than her husband, took her husband's side, against her own daughter and her husband. Later events were to prove how right General Ocran and his wife were!

The professional bodies also went on strike in late 1977. Lawyers refused to go to court, which, therefore, could not sit. Nurses later joined in the strike, followed by doctors. The whole nation was rapidly grinding to a halt. In his desperation, Acheampong got some of the T.U.C. leaders on his side, with appointments to high State offices. But this move did not help much. The whole situation was so critical that the workers took actions themselves. Workers in the State oil refinery, the electricity corporation and public servants went on strike.

By mid-1978 Acheampong faced exhorbitant food prices, acute shortages of essential items, periodic shortages of petrol, the students at home on strike, thousands of people thrown into jail without trial for allegedly being saboteurs or anti-state elements; engineers, nurses, doctors, lawyers, all on strike. There was chaos and suffering everywhere. The people on strike were all taking a stand against the economic hardships, the mismanagement and corruption of the military régime and the crass failure in leadership by the military government.

They were also registering, in no uncertain terms, their abhorrence of Acheampong's determined efforts to extend his rule indefinitely. As stated earlier, when he came into office, Acheampong did not commit himself to a return to civilian rule, as the previous military régime had done. However, although he did not clearly commit himself to indefinite military rule, he niether gave any clear indications of any return to civilian rule in the foreseeable future. He kept playing a cat-and-mouse game till about late 1976, when he sprang before the nation the idea of Union Government. By this was meant a non-party Government, elected by civilians and made up of civilians, but with the Police and Army still represented. The whole clear idea was to ensure that whatever Government followed the military régime, Acheampong himself would stay as the President or Head of State.

Again, making use of the mass-media, especially the "Ghanaian Times", the régime launched a massive nationwide campaign to popularise the Union Government idea. The Ministry of Information worked overtime issuing pamphlets eulogising it. The press, radio and television were all marshalled towards the objective. Prominent people who supported Union Government were awarded with huge import licences, promotions, appointments or loans. Some prominent intellect- uals and politicians, bending over backwards in their praise of Union Government, even went as far as to claim that they had fathered "*the noble idea of Union Government*". How they could make such claims, when they knew or must have known the general opposition to the concept by practically the whole nation, beats the imagination. It also goes to show how omnipotent was Acheampong's hold of the State apparatus on the whole nation.

In a succession of events, a Constitutional Commission was set up, ostensibly to tour the country and assess public reaction to Union Government. To many serious observers of the political scene, it came as no surprise when this commission, chaired by the then Attorney-General came out with conclusions supporting Union Government. Quickly a referendum was held in May 1978, to determine the people's reaction to Union Government. Ingeniously, the Government, through intimidation, harrassment and imprisonment of its opponents, ensured that many of those opposed to "Union Government" did not register to vote. Rigging the referendum, the Government announced an unreasonably high percentage of support. This result deceived nobody, possibly not even themselves. Before the announcement of the results, the Electoral Commissioner, Justice Abban, in his determination and zeal to avoid the referendum being rigged, had been summarily dismissed, and serious attempts made on his life!

So anxious was the régime to rig the elections that in some cases, the votes announced as having supported "Union Government" were even more than the people registered and entitled to vote in the district!

Acheampong's anxiety about the future was not surprising. He faced the same problem as the coup-makers of 1966, which was to ensure that they were not succeeded by an unfriendly unsympathetic civilian Government, that might then try them for treason, with probably death sentences. In addition, there was the constant fear that such a civilian Government might probe their assets and wealth, and those of their wives, relatives and friends. For it was obvious to all that just as some of the civilian government members they had probed could not account for the sources of all their sudden wealth; likewise, they too on being probed, could simply not explain all the wealth acquired since the coup of 1972. The nightmarish situation for Acheampong and his men, facing a possible trial for treason would account for the irrational paranoid activities of Acheampong in 1977-78.

The first military régime contented itself with ensuring that an indemnity decree was issued, as part of the 1969 constitution, indemnifying them for all acts in connection with the coup and afterwards. They also were satisfied with handing over to a democratically elected civilian Government, which by a gentlemen's agreement, was not going to raise any academic questions about the legality of the coup, or worse yet, begin any embarrassing investigations and probes involving members of the outgoing régime. In fact, for the first military junta, these questions although real, were on the whole purely academic. Nobody seriously considered their being tried for treason, as the coup had been so popularly welcomed. Nor did anybody ever suggest that the gallant officers should be probed or investigated, as they had done to the previous Nkrumah ministers. Yet there were muted rumours that some of the "liberating" officers, in the process of liberating the nation from corruption, bribery, nepotism and other social evils, had become, alas, tainted with the same civilian diseases they came to eradicate.

For Acheampong, the questions about treason and corruption, were not at all academic or hypothetical. They were stark realities, which had to be dealt with successfully. His grand answer to them was to ingeniously devise a future form of successor civilian Government, in which he would still be in command, either as Chariman, or as a retired General-turned-civilian-President, on the lines of General Eisenhower. Indeed, he fancied being called popularly "IKE". However, unlike Eisenhower, he would ensure that there were no surprises. Hence the wild excitement in forcing the "Union Government" idea down the nation's throat, and the absurd rigging of the referendum.

Before, and during the period of the referendum, a few public figures, despite the grave risk to their lives and those of their relatives, came out boldly to challenge General Acheampong's dictatorship and his Union Government plans. At a time when highly-educated, prominent citizens, for the sake of high positions, ambassadorial appointments, promotions, import licences or loans, were gaily selling their consciences, it is salutary to record that in Ghana's hour of need, a few valiant public-spirited citizens put their consciences before their stomachs. They defied imprisonment, or in many cases, re-imprisonment, so that democracy might have a chance to thrive again in Ghana.

Prominent among these illustrious citizens of the nation were Dr K. Safo-Adu, J.H. Mensah, Paa Willie, G.W. Armartefio, Prof. Adu Boahen (Professor of History, Ghana University, Legon), Chief Dombo, Jato Kaleo, R.R. Amponsah, Sam Okudjeto, Harry Sawyerr, Peter Adjetey. Their selfless stand for democracy and human rights is an outstanding feature of a generally depressing picture of obsequiousness, boot-licking, unashamed grovelling, with all moral and ethical standards thrown overboard. Nor can one forget the bold stand of the Roman Catholic Church, which vociferously through its paper the "Standard" kept on openly warning Acheampong to desist from his activities, and consistently stood up for human rights, liberty and justice!

The general picture by mid-1978 may be gleaned from this excerpt from the "Ghanaian Times" of Monday January 1 1979, on the "*Political Scene in 1978*".

> Of the twenty-one years that the State of Ghana has been in existence, 1978 will, perhaps, go into history as the most turbulent, the most controversial and the most belligerent.
> It has been a turbulent year because it has, more than any other year, witnessed some of the most serious strikes in the nation's history – strikes by medical doctors, nurses, lawyers, lecturers, engineers, civil servants, journalists, workers of Electricity Corporations, to mention just a few.
> Some of these strikes were met with very stern reprisals like mass dismissals by the managements concerned or conditional reinstatement like making workers sign bonds of good behaviour.

In some cases committees of enquiry were appointed to investigate the grievances of striking workers; some of these committees are yet to submit the report of their findings.

That was not all. The demands of some of the strikers were so controversial that no government of the day would have given in. For example the university lecturers and students demanded the unequivocal resignation of the Acheampong government. Since neither side was prepared to give in the struggle went on.

Of course, it was the Union government proposal, the crippling of the economy and the corrupt system of allocating the nation's financial resources which sparked off this belligerent situation between the Government and the professionals who felt that they had a duty to draw the Government's attention to the 'dirty deals' going on in the society.

The fact was that almost the first half of the year saw the situation where a Ghanaian who had no contacts 'at the top' was doomed.

It is an open secret that young girls who on their own merits would not even qualify to be employed as clerks made fortunes overnight.

The years also saw the climax of the system of cheating popularly known s 'Kalabule". Market women were able to defy the police and the army, and dictate their own prices. It was a year which witnessed the 'death' of price control, and the birth of the system of 'buy if you can.'

All these economic turmoils became possible and perhaps easy because Acheampong's government was more concerned with winning the March 30 Referendum on Union Government than anything else.

The public debate on Union government took a very dramatic turn when an organization called People's Movement for Freedom and Justice (PMJF) came forward to oppose the Union Government idea.

Meanwhile, several pro-UNIGOV groups had mushroomed 'out of nowhere' to 'educate' the people on the ideas of UNIGOV.

Several non-political organizations contributed to the public

155

debate on this 'new system of government', and the churches were no exception.

The controversial 'Pastoral Letter' issued by the Catholic Bishops of Ghana sparked off a hot debate from certain quarters, and brought a question mark on the real issue of freedom of expression.

Besides the Pastoral Letter, statements were issued by bodies like the Christian Council of Ghana, the National Union of Ghana Students (NUGS), the Professionals Bodies Association of Ghana, the Ghana Trades Union Congress, either for or against the proposal.

So it was that the Referendum on Union Government proposal was held on March 30 and 'Yes' was acclaimed the winner. But that was not the end.

With the 'Yes Victory' the Acheampong government felt it was no longer necessary to tolerate any more open opposition to the proposal. Consequently all organisations which directly or indirectly opposed the Unigov proposal were disbanded and declared illegal.

To escape arrest, several people, mostly the intellectuals opposed to the Union Government, fled the country and went into voluntary exile.

Even though the proposal was supposed to have found favour with the majority of the Ghanaian electorate through the referendum results, paradoxically, as the 'Yes Victory' on March 30 which occasioned the downfall of Acheampong and all that he stood for?

Tensions rose high as certain identifiable groups like the University Students, the Professional Bodies, became determined to use all the means at their disposal to bring down the S.M.C. Government.

Arrests and detention without trial were some of the means of silencing all the opponents.

That General Kutu Acheampong, with all the available machinery at his disposal could not fool all the people all the time was clearly demonstrated on July 5, when the Union Government General had the shock of his life. On that day, General Ignatius Kutu Acheampong was hustled out of power by his own colleagues. It was strange but true.

156

Following the announcement of the rigged referendum results, the régime started mass arrests of most of its opponents in April 1978. The lucky ones fled the country, taking refuge in Togo, Ivory Coast, Nigeria and Britain. Those not so lucky went to prison, without trial. Acheampong's régime was determined to make a final onslaught on all opposition. Having won a pyrrhic victory with its referendum results, Acheampong felt that his headaches were not over. To assuage public demands for civilian rule, more changes were made in the Government, bringing in more hand-picked favourites of the Head of State, but, alas, the régime's credibility gap had become too deep to be filled by cosmetic changes in the Government. The fact that, in addition to the estimated 4000 detainees, the régime had arrested a further 300 people, including 24 prominent citizens, among them former ministers of the régime overthrown in 1972, could not be hidden.

As a result of the chaotic state of the nation, and following interminable negotiations between Acheampong and the leaders of the professional bodies, nurses, workers, students, Acheampong announced a return to civilian rule scheduled for Jun-July 1979. *Even he had, at long last, to concede that there is a limit to how long one can rule with the gun, a whole nation against its will.* During these negotiations between him and the leaders of the professional bodies, it became evident that Acheampong was determined, in any way possible, to stay in power. He even threatened that if they wanted him to rule like Idi Amin of Uganda he was prepared to do so. But these threats had by now lost their potency and strength. Some of the civilian negotiators e.g. Sam Okudzeto, actually challenged him to shoot them. In the end some of them were manhandled by the security forces, and detained.

Previous to these negotiations, Bishop Andoh and other

prominent church leaders had in 1977 and again in 1978 made determined efforts to steer Acheampong from further catastrophe, by imploring him to resign gracefully. He scoffed at all these efforts. He felt that having survived several coup attempts, especially in 1972-74, to dislodge him, he could weather the impending dark and heavy storms. Even when, in 1976, two major attempts were made from the Army itself by senior colleagues to force him to resign, they had been defeated, through last-minute leaks by a couple of officers, who were more interested in their promotion prospects than the state of the nation. They had informed Acheampong, who had summarily "retired" the plot-leaders concerned.

However, while it appeared that all efforts to remove Acheampong might not succeed, it equally appeared that Acheampong himself could find no ways and means of avoiding the evident drift towards catastrophe and oblivion. He seemed to have exhausted all his options. He had tried detentions, imprisonment, harrassment, bribery of opponents, but none seemed to provide the desired results. The schools, colleges and universities were still shut. The strikes and demonstrations by nurses, doctors, lawyers, engineers, and other public servants still showed no signs of ending by early 1978. To pre-empt any major, serious move from the officers, Acheampong shrewdly, in June 1978, at the height of the nation-wide strikes, demonstrations and public outcry against his régime, sent a strong, secret memo to the members of the military junta, (S.M.C.) and other battalion commanders. In it he reviewed the whole chaotic, economic and political mess and turmoil in the country, and rhetorically asked *why* it was that the régime which had been hailed in January 1972 as having come to save the country, should now be saddled with so many difficulties and such all-pervading unpopularity, to the extent that people were openly hooting and booing at soldiers in uniform. Anguishing about the stark realities facing the régime, he invited his colleagues to help find solutions to these national problems, and to restore the tarnished image of the Armed Forces.

But unknown to Acheampong, long before he despatched his *memo* a growing number of senior officers, witnessing the country's rapid breakdown, had come to a firm conclusion that there would be no hope of healing the internal divisions in the country, or restoring the economy, so long as Acheampong had reached the point where he could not climb down without a heavy loss of face, nor could he carry on either. It had become evident to many people that he was no longer wanted as a leader, and that he had failed to "redeem" the nation, as he had promised in January 1972.

On July 5 1978, the date scheduled for a special meeting of the military régime (S.M.C.) and the senior officers, constituting the Military Advisory Council (M.A.C.), with Acheampong as Chairman of the whole meeting, to discuss his memo and other major, national affairs on the agenda, the impossible became possible. For a couple of days before the meeting, a handful of courageous and determined senior officers, deeply concerned about the state of affairs in the country, had decided to act on Acheampong's memo. Led by Brigadier N.A. Odartey-Wellington, then First Infantry Brigade Commander, they had approached the then Chief of Defence Staff, General Akuffo, about their conviction that Acheampong had to be forced to resign, and that until he went, there would be no hope for the nation. Akuffo and the Director of Military Intelligence agreed with the plan to remove Acheampong as Head of State, as soon as the scheduled meeting began. Senior colleagues of theirs who were known to be more pro-Acheampong than patriotic, such as the Army Commander, Bob Kotei, were carefully kept out of the plot. In effect, the whole plot was very simple. A resignation statement was secretly prepared and typed. Acheampong was to be asked to sign it during the meeting and if he refused, would have to be dealt with "militarily".

As he entered the conference room in Burma Camp on July 5 1978, Acheampong sensed something uneasy. The meeting appeared larger than was normally the case. He jokingly remarked that it appeared to be "an invasion". Unknown to him, but pre-arranged between the palace-coup organisers, his armed bodyguard were diverted from him and disarmed by the Military Intelligence. At the meeting, he was immediately confronted by his senior colleagues who argued that from their analysis of the country's situation of shortages, mounting inflation, unemployment, strikes and demonstrations, and in response to his own memo, they had come to a conclusion that the only solution was for him to resign forthwith. Odartey-Wellington spoke, so did the C.D.S., Akuffo, and others, especially the younger battalion commanders, constituting the Military Advisory Council. As the debate got more acrimonious, Acheampong shrewdly pleaded to be given more time to think, and to be allowed to give his final answer at the next meeting.

After six and a half years of dealing with him, his colleagues had come to know him too well. They suspected that it would be one more of his treacherous ploys to get out of their clutches, go out, and have announced immediately on the state radio their own immediate "retirement" or "dismissal", for "attempted coup or revolt". As such, they insisted on his signing immediately their prepared statement. Seeing that his opponents were serious, Acheampong tried to bluff his way through by refusing to resign. He was then threatened with a pistol! He agreed to sign the statement, but asked to be left alone with the members of the military junta. The rest, therefore, withdrew and after a few hours of heated argument, Ignatius Kutu Acheampong gave in. He bargained with his colleagues not to be probed or disgraced, that none of his assets would be confiscated, that he

160

would not be imprisoned! Appropriately assured, he duly signed the resignation statement to the effect that in the interests of national unity and peace, and to heal the divisions in the country and ensure stability, he was resigning as the Head of State, and retiring from the Army, with immediate effect.

Throughout the meeting, his closest friends and supporters, including some who had been with him in Government since 1972, refused to challenge his removal. They kept mute. One of them, in an effort to slip out, ostensibly to put his men on the alert, but rather suspected of trying to go out to organise resistance against the palace-coup, was prevented from going out of the meeting.

After Acheampong had signed the statement, it was decided to send him by helicopter to the Presidential Lodge at Akosombo, overlooking the Volta River. But Acheampong pleaded to go by car, as he was not keen on helicopter flights. So, by noon on 5 July 1978, he was driven under escort to Akosombo. Immediately it was announced in the afternoon news on the State Radio. A stunned, but unsympathetic nation thus heard that General Ignatius Kutu Acheampong had been removed by his officers, and had been replaced by the Chief of Defence Staff (C.D.S.) Lt. General Akuffo.

Thus, by the time of his fall, Acheampong had been in office for six and a half years. Like Nkrumah, he had failed to realise that a national leader whose support is based on his control of the police and the military intelligence, terrorising so-called "opposition groups" and not on the free will of the governed, will sooner or later, come to grief. The history of Ghana, if not indeed that of the whole world, clearly tells us that such a leader is likely to die by the hands of the very same strong-arm security forces that he relies upon to prop his régime, against the people's will. By the time the Redeemer learnt this hallowed lesson of modern history, it was too late. The rise and fall of

161

Ignatius Kutu Acheampong vividly reminds one of the Biblical saying: *"They who live by the sword shall die by the sword."*

Following the removal of Acheampong, changes in command at the highest level in the Ghana Armed Forces became necessary. Firstly, the former C.D.S., Lt. General Akuffo now became the Head-of-State and Commander in Chief of the Armed Forces. He was replaced as C.D.S. by Major General Joshua Hamidu, a brilliant, dedicated and honest officer, who, as Director of Military Intelligence in the Busia régime (1969 – January 1972) had been duped and out-manoeuvred by Acheampong, when he was planning his coup. Previously, the Army Commander, then Bob Kotei, a protégé of Acheampong, was promoted C.D.S. but "retired" a few weeks later. Brigadier Odartey Wellington now became the new Army Commander, a position which he was to hold with much distinction and honour right to his last hour, defending the honour of the Army and the nation.

Acheampong, however had laid such a firm foundation for a future revolution that probably nothing could have prevented that event from taking place. It was then common knowledge, even to unconcerned observers that the former Head of State and some of his officers, both within the barracks and outside, but especially the latter, were deeply involved in bribery and corruption, misappropriation of State funds, nepotism and open plundering of the State coffers. The evidence for these suspicions, views and rumours was plain for all to see. There could be no reasonable explanation for the large and luxurious houses mushrooming in the best residential areas of the capital and other cities, which were known to belong to certain officers, mostly those seconded into civilian jobs, a few of whom were still in the Armed Forces. Nor could the ordinary man find any explanation for the brand new Mercedez-Benz cars flying all over Accra, or the large farms and businesses known to be owned, directly or indirectly, by certain serving or retired officers and their wives or friends. It was the flamboyant display of conspicuous consumption at a level unparalleled in Ghana's history, which was to lead to the doom of the officers concerned.

As the financial and social backgrounds of all these new rich officers were known, their sudden transformation from men of modest or very limited means into rich and affluent men, could not but set tongues wagging, among a population in which most of the people are poor. To cap it all, the display of opulence by the few was contemporaneously taking place, with the existence of abject poverty and deprivation in the vast majority of the population. Continuous public appeals by the former to the latter for belt-tightening and personal sacrifices in the national interest, were not only naive and hollow, but also hypocritical and counter-productive. They only served to annoy the public and to make them ask, of course, privately, embarrassing questions about the wealth of the new rich.

Acheampong, by his clever policy of giving as many civilian jobs as possible to officers and men loyal to him, had directly created a big gap in the Armed Forces. As the numbers of civilian posts, by the very nature of things, were limited, it meant that only the favoured and fortunate few could get civilian jobs, which brought with them heavy allowances, perks, and social opportunities, plus a huge opportunity to make fortunes through graft, for those corruptly inclined. While the vast majority of officers and men who stayed in barracks and did not get civilian jobs had to make ends meet as before, their lucky counterparts became an envied class, not in arms, but in money. By so deeply and heavily politicising the Army, Acheampong effectively created two classes in the Army – the hapless majority, sitting it out in barracks and the lucky minority, busily doing civilian jobs outside, and reaping the benefits of the coup, directly or indirectly. The constant rumours that their soldier-turned-civilian administrators were greedily and uncontrollably acquiring more and more property, added to the envy of the majority.

It would be worth mentioning here that in April 1967 one of the major reasons which Lieutenant Arthur had given for his abortive coup, was allegedly the promotions which some of the senior officers had given themselves, following the coup of 1966, and also the feeling that the few officers seconded to civilian jobs were rumoured to be feathering their own nests. But the first military régime deployed so few officers into civilian jobs, that these accusations were generally ignored by the public as unsubstantiated. That these accusations, unfounded as they generally were, had been made at all, is an indication of the grave danger which a military régime runs as it gets more and more deeply involved in civilian affairs and administration.

On the political and economic scene, Akuffo inherited a country whose economy was practically bankrupt. Inflation was running at about 120 per cent per annum. Unemployment was about 50 per cent. The cedi's real and accepted value was about one-tenth its official rate of exchange. There was acute shortage everywhere of all essential food items, drugs, medicines, spare parts and tyres. Hospitals, colleges and schools, universities and factories had closed because of strikes against Acheampong.

Credits from the West had long stopped, and the country was not in a position to pay cash for its imports as it could do in 1972-75. Due to social deprivations, burglary, robbery-with-violence and prostitution had reached high levels, causing concern to many people.

Education and excellence had been drastically reduced in public estimation, as persons not so well-endowed became rich and opulent, through shady business practices, at the expense of the educated, the honest and the upright. This was the general legacy that six and a half years of the Redeemer's rule left General Akuffo, his successor. It was a task serious enough to daunt the most determined and fearless.

Chapter 9 – The Writing on the Wall

When Lt Gen F.W.K. Akuffo, took over from Acheampong as the new Head of State on July 5 1978, there were four major problem areas with which he had to grapple immediately. Although his intervention had averted a highly explosive situation from blowing up, he had intervened just a bit too late. The rot which had set in the politics of the state, had gone so far and so deep, that even Akuffo, with all his charm, and his national reputation for fair-play, boldness and discipline, could really do very little about the nation's problems. And the four major problem areas were first the Army, second, the chaotic economic situation, third, the constitutional future of the country; and finally, the fate of General Acheampong, his immediate predecessor.

By the time of his assumption of power, the Army, although still loyal to the military junta, was in a highly restive state. There were many in the Army who were rather disillusioned and disappointed with the poor performance of Acheampong, and wanted a clean sweep with the past, and an immediate return to barracks. A few, still loyal to Acheampong, were unhappy about his overthrow and dismissal. As such, Akuffo gave this problem in the Army priority attention. Apart from his nation-wide radio and television broadcast to the nation on taking over, he also addressed officers and other ranks, in the Armed Forces, giving the reasons for Acheampong's overthrow and the justification for the palace coup which he and his small band of colleagues had effected.

The *raison d'etre* for the mini coup was generally accepted by the overwhelming majority of the members of the Armed Forces, including some of the closest, former collaborators of Acheampong. However, the very actions which Akuffo took to placate the Army and keep it as a non-political, cohesive military organisation only fuelled grumblings and discontent in the Army.

Although Akuffo, on taking over, had effected minor changes in the new military junta, now called S.M.C. 2, the very fact that many of the former colleagues of Acheampong remained on the junta, and in various government positions, led to the asking of very embarrassing questions, especially by the Junior Officers. Their argument was simple and straightforward. If Acheampong had been removed because of all the charges and accusations of corruption, one-man rule, despotism, immorality, misappropriation of state funds, breaches of the rules of collective government, then why keep in the new, reconstituted government some of the same people who had aided and abetted Acheampong's alleged crimes, right from the coup day in January 1972? How, they argued, could you remove Acheampong, and not his active collaborators of the past? There could not be any definitive explanations or answers to such questions.

Akuffo, therefore, toured the different units during July to September 1978, justifying his actions of 5 July 1978, but unable (satisfactorily) to answer these questions, especially from the junior ranks and those senior officers who had not enjoyed the benefits of holding civilian jobs. The standard excuse and answer that continuity and experience were needed in the high command of the Army, and that the organisation would be demoralised and disorganised if all the Acheampong senior officers were to be removed, did not cut much ice with the vitriolic critics of the new régime. They considered as merely cosmetic Akuffo's attempt to revamp the image of the new régime by dropping Acheampong's notorious Army Commander, Bob Kotei, and a few others. They wanted a drastic removal of the whole lot who had been close associates of Acheampong. This really could not be done. If the logic of the argument were to be carried to its conclusion, it would have meant removing the new Head of State himself, Akuffo, who had also been a close associate of Acheampong from the days of the coup. It would have meant a drastic and wholesale dismissal of a high number of senior officers.

There was also another source of mutinous rumblings in the Army. This was the question of the future of those senior officers who had been seconded to civilian jobs in the Acheampong period of 1972-78. That some of them were corrupt and dishonest, greedy and avaricious, was generally suspected and taken for granted by the public long before the revolution of June 1979. As civilian rule approached, it was decided by the military régime that such officers could, if they wished, revert to their army positions, promotions and careers as if they had never left for the civilian jobs. This angered immensely those serving officers who had all along taken unkindly to the perks and advantages, social and financial, which these officers had gained by being seconded to civilian positions, to the great disadvantage of their contemporaries and colleagues who remained in barracks. Such anger and bitterness were to lead to demands by the disaffected officers and men that these returning officers should be probed and investigated, as to the sources of the assets of themselves and their families, acquired during their period of civilian assignment.

Since the coup of February 1966, the precedent has been set in Ghana that the outgoing administration should be probed by the incoming administration and asked to complete questionnaires and forms about the incomes and assets, property, cars, etc., of their wives, themselves, and their children. After the coup against Nkrumah in February 1966, this national exercise in humiliation and disgrace had been done by the first military junta against the Nkrumah ministers and top officials. The results established corruption at a disgustingly high level against most of them.

When the military régime handed over power to civilian Government of Busia, no such investigations were held against them. Finally, after Acheampong's coup of January 1972 a similar exercise was held against the Busia men. Now, in July 1978, the military junta was seriously proceeding with consti-tutional plans to hand over to a future civilian government. And there was hence the vociferous request by many soldiers and officers that their colleagues returning to barracks to rejoin them should cleanse themselves by facing similar commissions or committees of enquiry. This demand was made verbally and in diverse ways to the new military régime as the best means of clearing the Army of charges and rumours of bribery and corruption which were being blatantly levelled at them by the public in the latter stages of Acheampong's rule. The military critics of their contemporary military-civilian colleagues felt that they should be accountable to the nation as a whole or at least to their military comrades.

The embarrassment and complications which such deep investigations and public probes could produce for the military junta can well be imagined. There was always the likelihood that during such probes one piece of evidence could lead to another and ultimately set in motion a train of events which might destroy the image, name and reputation of the officers concerned and others and, by implication, that of the whole Army. The more foresighted of these military-civilian officers cleverly "retired" or resigned from the Army voluntarily, just before or after Acheampong's overthrow. But the majority stayed on, with cherished hopes of resuming their military careers, under the umbrella and blessing of a new, non-probing and friendly civilian administration of the immediate future. Thus the strenuous demand by Acheampong and certain officers, before and after July 1978, that a future civilian government should still allow for representation by the Army and Police, made perfect sense. Only under such a constitutional arrangement could their own *fortunes* and *lives* be assured of any safety and guarantee. Such was the nature of the military problem which Akuffo had to face from his colleagues.

Tall, handsome, and fiercely-moustached, Akuffo came to his new office with a fairly widespread reputation for honesty. He was not known to possess itching palms, and his assumption of office was widely acclaimed by the public. But Akuffo, unlike previous Ghana "liberators" or "redeemers", strenuously discouraged all the usual, traditional adulations, telegrams, resolutions and demonstrations of support from chiefs, trade unionists, students, senior civil servants, farmers, and market women. Frequently accused of being stand-offish and aloof, he tried to live and govern above the usual, petty squabbles, rumours, accusations and counter-accusations vigorously rife in Ghana politics. He set himself a definite assignment, the immediate return to civilian rule, and he approached that task with single-minded dedication.

The other major problem area confronting Gen Akuffo, was the messy and intractable state of the economy. There was very little that he could do to salvage six and a half years of Acheampong's erratic economic policies which had brought the country to the point of bankruptcy. In international financial circles, Ghana was treated like a pariah, for it had become a country saddled with immense debts and little hope of their being repaid. To cap it all, it was ruled by a man whose intemperate language in public was such as to make the country a high-risk area for foreign investments or loans. The estimated inflation rate of 150-200 per cent, the chronic deficit in the balance of payments, the abnormally high level of unemployment, the black market, the dangerously high cost of living, which made a loaf of bread cost as much as a worker's whole day's pay, were symptoms of an economy which was almost moribund.

What could Akuffo do about these problems which had defeated successive civilian and military Governments in Ghana since Independence in March 1957? First of all, he put an immediate end to the wild, anti-Western (especially anti-American) public pronouncements and extravagant statements of his predecessor. He was shrewd and intelligent enough to realise that any Ghana Government which is outspokenly anti-West should not expect much economic aid or assistance from the West. I am not stating a necessarily pro-Western stance here. I am merely stating what, in my view, is mere common sense! It would be irrational and unrealistic for the leader of a country to be violently anti-Communist, and at the same time expect largesse and hefty economic assistance from the Communist East.

Akuffo realised Ghana's economic position, its deep historic and economic ties with the West, and quickly set about mending the fences and bridges which had been so crudely and unnecessarily broken by his predecessor. In fact, by March 1979, only eight months after his installation into office as the Head of State of Ghana, Akuffo, had been so successful in renewing the old ties of friendship with Ghana's traditional allies that he was scheduled for an official visit to Britain, in that month. Disappointingly, the pressures of local problems and difficulties forced him to postpone that visit indefinitely. His rational, pragmatic approach to Ghana's economic problems bore ample dividends, and he was able, within the short time he was in office, to arrange sizeable foreign assistance for Ghana to bail the tottering economy.

The notorious S.U.L. system of importing goods whereby people or organisations with external funds were allowed to bring in goods without the usual import licence, was abolished immediately by Akuffo's new, clean-sweeping régime. As soon as the S.U.L. system was abolished, the black market rate for the cedi fell drastically by over fifty per cent, for there was now less demand for foreign exchange than when the S.U.L. system was in operation.

To supplement the action taken in abolishing S.U.L., the régime rigorously curtailed the numbers of people flying, regularly and frequently, overseas. This was done to conserve accutely needed foreign exchange, at a time when hospitals were short of drugs and schools short of exercise books, stationery, and other educational items. Also, the travel-allowance for overseas travel, per person, was reduced from 400 dollars to 100 dollars. The Akuffo régime appeared determined to rejuventate an almost dying economy, to a semblance of some good health. And the measures which it took on the economic field endeared it to the masses, although not to the few greedy and rapacious traders and business people who, by their activities, had dealt a death-blow to the country.

Akuffo effected a re-organisation of the commodity distribution system. Until then, under Achaempong, essential commodities were mostly distributed by a few shops and firms, either owned by friends and favourites, or by the U.T.C., C.F.A.O. But these firms were very limited in the allocation of import licences to import goods. In a number of cases, larger companies received even less import licences than individuals or small firms who were in the good books of Acheampong. By trying to remove such blatant injustices and anomalies, Akuffo effected a wider and more equitable distribution of food to the rural and remote areas of the country.

Akuffo set up a number of Commissions of Enquiry to review Government contracts, loans and financial transactions undertaken in the Acheampong régime. But to a highly suspicious and cynical public, the results and conclusions of these investigations did not come as a surprise. In one way or another, the reports fully confirmed the general suspicions of the public.

The major contribution of Akuffo towards ameliorating the severe economic conditions in the country was acting on the advice of local and international economics experts to drastically devalue the cedi. All along his period of government, Acheampong had toyed with the idea of devaluing the currency. But he had always pulled from the brink when it came to taking the final decision. He remembered too well that Busia's devaluation of the cedi in December 1971 was one of the major reasons which he himself had given for his action in forcibly overthrowing that Govenment. As such, right to the day of his political demise he refused to devalue, as the economic situation clearly demanded. Akuffo, by approving the devaluation of the cedi, thus made another major break with his predecessor's régime.

The devaluation plus the abolition of the S.U.L. system, restored a great measure of sanity to the chaotic financial system in the country. At the same time it brought the official value of the cedi nearer the black-market rate, thus drastically minimising speculation and the constant run on the currency. In addition, the régime tried to check the smuggling of gold, diamonds and cocoa from the country to surrounding African states, and overseas. The measures against smuggling, although highly publicised, were not very successful, for in some cases, the same officers and men required to carry them out had been the same people responsible for such assignments under Acheampong.

Apart from these economic measures which the Akuffo régime

took, there were the usual public exhortations to the masses to tighten their belts, sacrifice, work harder, etc. As under previous régimes, these exhortations were not taken seriously by the public, who had come to treat such public statements as mere propaganda exercises meant to cajole a gullible public.

The third major problem for Akuffo was a constitutional one. At the time Acheampong was forced to resign, a referendum had just been held, asking the electorate whether they supported the idea of 'Union Government' or not. The 'YES' vote which the Government announced in April 1978 was taken by many people as rigged and incorrect. However, acting on the so-called verdict of the people in favour of Union-Government, the Acheampong régime had set up a so-called Constituent Assembly to draw a constitution for the country on the basis of Union Government. This Assembly which was elected from various professional, trade, and social groups in the country, was heavily weighted in favour of Union Government supporters. It was while this very Assembly was sitting that Acheampong was dismissed. He had, in May 1978, after considerable pressure from the professional bodies, students, and workers, agreed to a return to civilian rule by July 1979, with free elections being held in June 1979. In fact, this was the condition by which the professional bodies, nurses, doctors, workers, had agreed to call off their nationwide strikes. As such, by the time Akuffo took over, the ground for a return to civilian rule had already been prepared on the basis of 'Union Government'.

Akuffo inherited a situation where the Army was split on this major constitutional issue. Those in the Army who had *not* gone out on civilian jobs (the majority) were in favour of an immediate and unconditional return to civilian rule, complete with the jettisoning of the whole idea of Union Government, which they clearly saw as unacceptable to the vast majority of the people. On the other hand, many of the officers who had done civilian jobs were inclined to support Union Government. In this view, they were openly and heartily supported by a number of prominent politicians and chiefs, among whom were a good number who had failed to obtain parliamentary seats in the 1969 General Elections. Also in favour of Union Government were a few lawyers and doctors who, as a tiny minority among their professional collegues, had refused to join the nation-wide strike of professional people against the Acheampong regime. Akuffo thus took over at a time when this public debate over the country's future Constitution was going on vigorously. Many people, especially the professional bodies and students, were not prepared to accept anything short of a complete, unconditional return to civilian rule.

The arrest, in April 1978, of many professional people and politicians, mostly from the Busia régime, had only exacerbated the situation. From July 1978 till about the end of the year, General Akuffo appeared to have toyed with the possibility of a return to civilian rule, on the basis of Union Government. But the forces against him, not only in the Armed Forces, but also in the whole country, were too strong. To register in no uncertain terms their strong opposition to Union Government and also to press for improved conditions of service, many civil servants and others in the public sector went on strike in November 1978.

Suspecting that old politicians and other professional people, were behind the nation-wide strike, Akuffo announced a State of Emergency on November 6, restricting further the "human rights" of the people. Furthermore, he allowed publication of the reports of the various committees of enquiry, into the assets of the Busia ministers.These reports had been ready since 1973, but for one volume on Busia and a couple of ministers, had not been published by the Acheampong régime, as a means of keeping a psychological hold on the political activities of the ministers and politicians involved. By authorising the release to the press of these reports, the régime effectively diverted, at least temporarily, the attention of the public from the current political and economic problems, to the favourite, old, political subject of consuming interest to the Ghanaian public – the corruption of ministers and other politicians.

Meanwhile the pressure from the Armed Forces, especially from the younger members, for a quick, unconditional return to civilian rule without any commitment to Union Government, continued. By December 1978, after a number of pro and anti-Union Government statements, the Government settled for a complete, unconditional return to civilian rule, without any commitment to Acheampong's Union Government proposition. The Constituent Assembly brought in more persons whose anti-Union Government views were known and was authorised to discuss the whole question of a future constitution for Ghana. They were thus mandated to draw a new Constitution for Ghana to replace the 1969 Constitution which had been suspended by Acheampong in 1972.

While these discussions for a new Constitution continued, preparations for the holding of free genuine elections went ahead. Firstly, General Akuffo, as Head of State on 31 December 1978, made his first New Year broadcast to the nation. In it he appealed to the nation to be more hardworking and law-abiding and to help the economic reconstruction of the economy. Significantly, he lifted the State of Emergency which had been imposed on 6 November 1978. Furthermore, the ban on politics and political activities which had been imposed by Acheampong, since his overthrow of the civilian régime of Dr Busia, in January 1972, was lifted. These measures, he said, were taken so that *all* people would feel free to organise themselves in preparation towards the general elections scheduled to be held in June 1979. To ensure that these elections did not bring back the past political rancour, a Political Parties Decree was issued setting out the conditions for participation in the elections. The names and symbols of previous parties could not be used in the June elections. The names of 105 persons who, as a result of adverse findings made against them by commissions or committees of enquiry which were set up since the coup of 1966, could no longer hold public office, including standing for elections, were published. Immediately, a public row began over the disqualification of these 105 persons. Admittedly, after the coup of 1966, a number of former prominent politicians had been similarly disbarred from holding public office, only their names were not specifically set out by the Attorney General's office, and it was left to the public to take legal action to politically immobilise these people.

This had led to a number of contentious and frivolous actions. In order to avoid a repetition of that situation, the Attorney-General's office had itself prepared the names of these 105 persons from all régimes since 1966, who, in their opinion, had had adverse findings made against them. The trouble then arose over whether these affected persons should be allowed a right of appeal, which had not been accorded to the ministers and officials of the Nkrumah régime. After considerable heart-searching the Government decided that *all* those so affected, from whatever régime, should be allowed to appear before a review tribunal, headed by a High Court judge, to review their cases. This fair solution seemed to have satisfied the public.

With the lifting of the ban on politics on 1 January, 1979, it became evident that a number of former military-civilian commissioners and officials, who had held senior governmental positions in the military régimes of 1966-69, and 1972-72, also entertained political ambitions. They were no longer on the active list in the Forces, and, therefore, could stand for election, under the new electoral decree. The very fact that they had not been probed or investigated, as had been done to all former ministers and top party officials, appeared to be unfair in the eyes of many people. The argument was that if civilian ministers are probed, why not the military, especially as the latter had set themselves up as paragons of virtue and honesty? Again, after much anguish, and public and press argument, the régime decided to set up another review committee headed by a senior judge, to investigate the assets of all those members of the former régimes who wished to enter public life and had not already been probed and cleared by previous commissions or committees of enquiry.

In the opinion of many, this review tribunal was not as rigorous and penetrating as that which the civilian politicians had had to face in 1966, and 1972. However, the fact that it was set up at all was an attempt by the military régime to ensure that some semblance of equity and justice was applied to all aspiring politicians and office-holders. The politicians in 1966 and 1972 had had to fill in long, exhaustive questionnaires about their income, since their earliest working days, and give all details about their assets, wealth, property and those of their wives and children. They had to do it while in prison, in a state of shock and confusion, without any opportunity of consulting family and friends, or documents. At least, the people who faced the enquiry in 1978-79 had the opportunity of operating from the comfort of their homes, without any police or special branch harrassment or intimidation, and with full recourse to family conversations, records and documents.

As a further step towards a return to civilian rule, the régime revamped its image still further. When it took over in July 1978, it had replaced some of Acheampong's men and appointed its own to replace them. It had also appointed more civilians to replace some of the military-civilian Commissioners and officials. In January 1979, it went one step further. The military in the administration, with the exception of the Commissioner for Trade and Tourism, and a few others, were replaced by responsible, respected, well-known civilians. Among the new appointees was the new Foreign Minister (Mrs Gloria Nikoi), who thus became the first Ghanaian woman to hold that post; Mr Justice A.N.E. Amissah, a retired Appeal Court Judge, who replaced an Acheampong appointee, Dr G. Korangteng Addo, as Attorney-General. His predecessor had been a strong and open advocate (as Attorney-General) of the discredited Union-Government project, and indeed was Chairman of the Committee which toured the country in 1977 to collect and collate nation-wide opinions on the concept of a non-party form of Government. His Committee had produced a report claiming that the majority of the people favoured and liked Union Government. But many people, especially among the professionals, felt that the report was not worth the paper on which it was written.

Consequently, when the new régime, after much vacillation, decided to reject the idea of Union Government, its Attorney-General, was left in a limbo. In a major public speech at Kumasi University in January 1979, he reiterated his view that the country was not ready for multi-party politics and that, in his opinion, the idea of Union Government was best for the country. On the speech being reported by the radio and television, he was dismissed immediately.

There was one major and difficult problem that continued ceaselessly to engage the attention and mind of Akuffo and his colleagues on the military junta, Supreme Military Council (No.2). It was a most delicate issue which simply would not go away – what to do with General Acheampong, the former Head of State? When he was removed, the nation had been told officially that he had resigned in the interests of unity, stability

180

and peace in the country. Subsequently in various public speeches, diverse allegations had been made directly or indirectly against him, as a way of explaining the current disastrous economic, political and social state. But to date, no specific charges had been made against him, nor were there any plans to bring him to trial. All that the public knew or got to know was that the former Head of State, was being shuffled from one prison to another, and that he was being comfortably looked after. Simultaneously, rumours in the press, and in other official and unofficial attacks on him, stated that Acheampong was being given preferential treatment in prison. Now, in a country where stealing even a little chicken meant a heavy sentence on prosecution to conviction, the public found it difficult to understand why Acheampong could not be brought to trial, or why none of his colleagues could be prosecuted.

Thus the whole march towards civilian rule was very much over-shadowed with the fate of Acheampong. The numerous parties which had sprung up since the ban on political activities was lifted on January 1 1979, continued to campaign. The Electoral Commissioner went ahead with the registration of voters, candidates, the establishment of polling centres, printing of ballot papers, symbols, etc., but the question of what to do with Acheampong still remained unresolved. Many of the politicians, unwilling to alienate some of his supporters were uncommittal about Acheampong's fate. This was especially the case with politicians who had enjoyed and benefitted from the bounty and largesse of Acheampong during his rule. However, a new party (The Popular Front Party) which succeeded the overthrown Busia régime made it abundantly clear that if they won, Acheampong would be subjected to due process of law for the coup of January 1972. Their action made sense, for they were the political and spiritual inheritors of the Progress Party Government of Dr Busia. Similarly, as Acheampong, throughout his period in office, had to rely more and more on the supporters of the past Nkrumah régime, as it would have been illogical to rely on the men of the Busia régime, these supporters of his could not really state that they would put him on trial, if they won the June elections. The best they could do was to keep quiet about Acheampong's fate and future.

Events now began to gallop at a tremendous speed. As nothing appeared to be done about the former Head of State, and with the elections and therefore, a return to civilian rule, rapidly approaching, rumours of all sorts thickened the air. It was said Acheampong had vast sums of money in Swiss Banks and overseas, and that he was refusing to surrender these to the new régime, until and unless members of that régime also disgorged their alleged funds in overseas banks, which he knew about. It was even rumoured that he had threatened to name certain powerful colleagues whose misdeeds and crimes he knew about and could substantiate in a court of law, should he be brought to trial, as many in the public were demanding. It was further rumoured that Acheampong claimed to have full dossiers on the criminal activities of his past and present colleagues, that these were being kept in the sealed vaults of overseas banks, and that he was waiting for the appropriate time to release them all on the country! Whether these rumours were true or false is really irrelevant. What is important is that they would inflame an inarticulate population, starved of definite, reliable information.

Finally, on 1 May, 1979, the Military Government, after much vacillation and heart-searching took a major, irreversible step towards solving the *Acheampong Question*. On that day, the military junta issued a decree enumerating a long series of very serious charges against the former Head of State. They ranged from political crimes to economic sabotage. They included charges of corruption, inefficiency, unwarranted interference in the State machine, and sexual immorality. Most of the charges were not only very serious, but carried the death penalty or long periods of imprisonment upon conviction after prosecution, under the prevailing laws of the land. Inexplicably, after detailing all these charges, the decree ended on a note of anti-climax. It stated that the Government had, in view of those allegations and charges, decided to strip the General of his military rank, dismiss him from the Army, freeze all his assets and those of his family, and *release* him from detention to be sent to his village in Ashanti, near Kumasi, to be confined.

After much indecision and vacillation, the Akuffo régime, in an effort to save its skin, had made a fatal mistake. For its solution of the Acheampong Question was no solution at all. That the man against whom so many serious charges had been made by the Government itself, should be *released* and allowed to go home without trial while at the same time, in the name of that Government, poor, simple people were being sent to prison for long sentences over such trivial offences as stealing a goat or sheep, or a few cedis, or forging "road-worthy" vehicle certificates, or fraudulently misappropriating a few thousand cedis of State funds, would beat the imagination of any normal, fair-minded human being. In fact, many people were so furious with the quixotic treatment of Acheampong by the military junta, that quickly the public joke grew that if it was a punishment and disgrace to be called a plain "mister", then at least seven million men in Ghana (about half the country's estimated population) were being unduly punished for no apparent crimes at all. What added insult to injury was the public knowledge that even before the official announcement of his release, Acheampong had been set free, and given a royal escort and welcome home by some of his friends and supporters.

Whatever Akuffo's motives in not bringing Acheampong to a public trial, can only be guessed. But he certainly, by this paradoxical move, undid himself.

Chapter 10 – The Revolution Starts

The whole nation was geared towards the General Elections on June 15, 1979. The politicians, candidates and their supporters were doing as much canvassing as possible. It all seemed to be progressing smoothly and properly towards Ghana's first, serious elections, since the General Elections of August 29 1969. It is true that the economic problems remained, but there was a general feeling that with a return to civilian rule, the new leaders would be able to sort out the country's problems. The whole administrative machinery of the nation was at a standstill, awaiting the outcome of the June 15 elections.

However, in all their private and public accusations of bribery and corruption, the plundering of the state coffers, malad-ministration, nepotism, misuse of state funds, which the public levelled against the Armed Forces, one issue on which practically all people agreed was that never again should the country be ruled by the military. From the point of view of the public, the seven years of military rule had been a long, bitter and disastrous period in the country's history. Indeed, it was the opinion of many fair-minded people that never in the nation's history had it experienced such a dangerously high-level of corruption, sheer abuse of power, moral laxity and spiritual decadence. Thus while opinions naturally differed on which political party was best-suited to replace the military régime of Acheampong, there was little controversy on the need for the military to leave the political scene as quickly as possible.

In a way, the oncoming General Elections, therefore, drew the attention of the public from their severe economic and social problems to that of the election campaign. It was all very lively and exciting. As in 1969, the state-controlled radio and television tried to be as non-partisan and impartial as possible, allowing open discussions on radio and television by the leaders or representatives of the various, major contending political parties. Equally, the state-owned Press (*Daily Graphic, Ghanaian Times*, the *Spectator* and *Mirror*), both in their reporting of news items, and in their political comments on events, succeeded generally in steering a middle course, and maintaining a spirit of independence from official control or influence from any of the major parties.

With the election campaign at its zenith the whole nation was stunned to learn from the State-radio, Radio Ghana, that there had been an attempted revolt or coup led by a certain Air Force Officer, Jerry John Rawlings*, and that the revolt had been quelled by forces loyal to the military régime. The announcement of the revolt and its failure in the morning of 15 May, 1979, came as a bolt from the blue. For the last thing that anybody in Ghana anticipated or wished for was another coup. With the return to civilian rule in July, 1979, so anxiously anticipated, it was difficult to see how another coup would materially improve the country's difficult economic and political situation.

What had happened was that Flight Lieutenant Jerry John Rawlings and a few followers in the Air-Force had pre-empted the return to barracks of the senior military officers by organising a revolt to force these officers to account to the nation for their assets, before a return to civilian rule. As the details of the revolt emerged, it became more and more evident that, although the reasons for the coup were justified, the whole interference with the smooth return to civilian rule was ill-timed, at best, and considered by many as not in the best interests of the country, although fully agreeing with his demands and objectives.

186

The actual mechanics of the Rawlings coup of 15 May, 1979 were fairly simple. They involved the capture of a number of senior military officers in the barracks, Burma Camp, Accra, as hostages, in order to pressurize the military government to accede to the demands of the "rebels". A few officers were thus captured in the early morning of 15 May, 1979, and kept as hostages at the Air-Force Base, Burma Camp. Rawlings, threatening to shoot these hostages, began to negotiate with the military junta through fellow-officers. The revolt collapsed within a matter of a few hours, due to the bravery and loyalty of the Commander of the Recce Regiment, Major Abdulai Sulemanu, a friend and contemporary of Rawlings. He was able personally to coax his friend out of the revolt, get the hostages released, some of them still in their early morning tennis attire and gymnastic suits. But the public at large supported Rawlings and overnight he became a national hero, talked of as a Messiah everywhere.

With the revolt ended, the military régime on May 28, 1979, set up a Military Tribunal to try Flight-Lieutenant Rawlings and his accomplices, on charges of conspiracy to commit mutiny and committing mutiny by violence.

With the Military Tribunal set up, the military régime of General Akuffo went about its business of governing the country. The whole abortive coup was treated by the régime, the politicians and some of the public generally, as a minor, insignificant episode of no substantial consequence. Despite massive press and public pressure that the rebels should not be tried, but should be dealt with under military law and executed, General Fred Akuffo, insisted that in fairness to the persons concerned, and in conformity to the best traditions of the Army, they should be given an open and fair trial, albeit according to military law. Hence, the convening of a tribunal, which first sat on May 29th 1979, with Colonel Enninful as President.

The details of the revolt remained sketchy until the beginning of the proceedings of the Tribunal. It was during the Attorney-General's opening address to the tribunal that the whole background and the reasons for the revolt began to emerge clearly. In view of the historic importance of what transpired at the Tribunal and in view of its relevance to the Ghana Revolution, it would be appropriate to set down here the salient points in the opening address of the Director of Public Prosecution, G.E.K. Aikins, at the Tribunal.

Following the stirring opening address by the Director of Public Prosecutions, the civilian audience at the trial became so excited with clapping and enthusiastic cheers for Rawlings and his co-accused, that at least on three occasions the President of the Tribunal, Col. Enninful, had to call vigorously for order and silence from the public; finally threatening to order them out if they continued to be so noisy and disruptive.

As the details of the attempted coup emerged from the eloquent address by the Director of Public Prosecution, more and more people began to sympathise with the aims of the conspirators. For if the Director of Public Prosecution was right in his statement of the alleged aims of the revolt then, according to many people, Rawlings had indeed brought to the fore and into the open what they had felt and known; that the military régime and its 'military-civilian' administrators were terribly corrupt, that they should indeed be probed by Commissions of Enquiry as had happened in 1966 and 1972 to civilian ministers, and that the preponderant role of Lebanese and Indians in the commerce and trade of the nation, to the disadvantage of indigenous Ghanaians, was unhealthy for the country's economy and unacceptable to the masses.

The trial of Rawlings and his co-accused, therefore, suddenly transformed them almost into national heroes. Nor was the feeling restricted to the civilian population. It was evident in the

Army also, many of whom were beginning to consider him as their unofficial spokesman. However, the general feeling in the country was that nevertheless, the whole revolt was ill-timed. Most people very much looked forward to the return to civilian rule.

Following the collapse of the Rawlings revolt on 15 May 1979, the military intelligence and security services launched an intensive search for the ring of conspirators, not yet arrested, who were behind the revolt or in any way connected with any budding revolt or coup against the Government

The painstaking assiduousness of the security services, especially the military intelligence, in their investigations soon established the existence of a cell or group of soldiers, mostly corporals, who met regularly in the rooms of one of their colleagues to discuss the current problems in the Army, in the country, and what to do about them. It was known, on highly reliable evidence that this group of conspirators, based in Burma Camp, was planning a coup to topple the military Government. It was therefore planned in late May 1979 by the Security Services to surprise them and arrest them at one of the irregular meetings.

Unfortunately for the military régime, but fortunately for the conspirators, the detachment of soldiers, who were sent to effect the arrest of the conspirators, under the command of a lieutenant, included a corporal, who was himself a member of the conspiracy! According to his account, when the arresting team reached the premises where his co-conspirators were holding their meeting, he asked the commanding officer to be allowed to go into the room first to surprise them, with the officer standing outside with his revolver at the ready, against any possible emergency. While inside the room, he briefed his comrades about their encirclement, convinced them to surrender, with the firm promise and assurance of their being subsequently released from guard-room, after their arrest, by himself and other comrades. They agreed, surrendered and were taken into custody by the corporal and his comrades. Independently, Rawlings and his men were being kept in custody outside Burma Camp, at the Special Branch Headquarters in Accra, a few hundred yards from Broadcasting House, the nerve-centre of the country's communication system.

Unknown to Rawlings and his men while they were in custody, this group of soldiers, had decided that following the failure of the Rawlings coup, on 15 May 1979, they would make another attempt, secure the release of all those soldiers in detention, and overthrow the military Government. Following the Director of Public Prosecution's stirring opening address during the trial of Rawlings and his men, the word had quickly got round that Flight-Lieutenant Rawling's coup, which had failed, had been aimed at corrupt senior officers, to the benefit of junior officers and other ranks in the Armed Forces. Rawlings had thus become a hero to the soldiers and junior officers, and they began to look to one exceptional officer risking his life for the non-officers. In an army of about 24,000 officers and men, with a ratio of one officer to about 100 non-officers the odds were heavily weighted against the officers in any confrontation.

On 30th May 1979, the Military Tribunal trying Flight-Lieutenant Rawlings and his group had adjourned at the request of their counsel, led by Barrister Adumua Bossman, President of the Ghana Bar Association. It had been successfully argued by them and been upheld by the Tribunal that they needed more time to consult their clients and to brief lawyers for those accused who still had no legal representation. The Tribunal was scheduled to resume sitting on 4th June 1979. There was no sign whatsoever that the Tribunal would not sit as scheduled.

But on the 4th June 1979, the new coup organisers struck. The Ghana Revolution had begun. In the early hours of 4 June 1979, under the overall command of Capt. Boakye Djan, the coup organisers broke into the Special Branch Headquarters where Flight-Lieutenant Rawlings was being held, forced their way into his cell and released him and his co-accused. Meanwhile, the other conspirators who were being held in Burma Camp, following their surprise and arrest by one of their colleagues, were released, as they had been promised.

After releasing Rawlings, the coup-makers ran with him to the nearby Broadcasting House. Thus it came about that while the morning commercial advertisements were being made on Radio Ghana at about 5.50 am, before the usual six o'clock morning news, the people who were listening to the announcements heard something unusual. The light music had been suddenly interrupted by the heavy panting of an unidentified man, who said nervously and incoherently words to the effect, 'The Supreme Military Council is overthrown . . . The Military Advisory Council is no more . . . Junior officers and other ranks of The Ghana Armed Forces have overthrown the corrupt, hypocritical Government of the Supreme Military Council . . .' Firing could be heard continuously in the background.

After this brief, incoherent, and puzzling statement, the radio broadcasts continued, not with the expected, usual six o'clock news, but with martial music. Firing could be heard in the background still. About half-an-hour later, a stunned nation heard on the radio the voice of a man who identified himself as Flight-Lieutenant Jerry John Rawlings, announcing to the nation his release from captivity by his comrades, and repeating the overthrow of the military junta by junior officers and other ranks of the Ghana Armed Forces. He asked the public to keep calm and stand by for further announcements. The military music was next resumed. The whole nation, preparing for election on 15 June 1979, was thrown into complete confusion. The man who was being tried for conspiracy, treason, mutiny, etc., had

191

broken from captivity, overthrown the Government, and put in jeopardy the very lives of the members of the military Government.

At about 9 am, the military music, and the recorded statement of Rawlings which was being played on the radio suddenly stopped. A voice identified himself as a Major from the Recce Regiment. He announced that the mutiny in the Armed Forces by a few disloyal elements had been successfully quelled by loyal forces and that the civilian population should keep calm, go about their usual business normally and 'leave it to the Armed Forces to sort things out'. The playing of military music was resumed for about another hour, when again it was interrupted. The voice of Major-General N.A. Odartey-Wellington, the Army Commander, was the next on the air. He confirmed that there had been a revolt in the Armed Forces by Flight-Lieutenant Rawlings and a few soldiers, and that it had been quelled. He passionately appealed to Rawlings and his band of followers to give up, meet him at an agreed military base near Accra, to 'sort out their alleged grievances and problems'. He assured them that there would be no arrests or victimisation, and that everything possible would be done to meet their demands and grievances. His recorded statement was broadcast at fifteen-minute intervals, interposed with military (and occasionally classical) music.

Meanwhile, outside the radio studios, a fierce battle was going on and occasionally one could hear the civilian broadcaster saying nervously, 'I am under fire! Shooting is going on . . .' For what had happened was that the soldiers who released Rawlings overpowered the military guards around the radio station, so that Rawlings could effect his broadcast of the coup. After that, the coup-makers had left for Burma Camp to oversee the coup, leaving behind a detachment of soldiers loyal to them to guard the radio station. These were subsequently over-powered and overrun by the Recce Regiment Officer and his armoured car detachment so that he could announce the quelling of the revolt by loyalist troops. It was while these troops with armoured cars were holding the radio station for and on behalf of the military Government, that the Army Commander, Major-General Odartey-Wellington, came in to make his announcement.

At the time of the Army Commander's broadcast Rawlings was in the air, with a few comrades, in one of the military jets, contacting Army units in different parts of the country, to inform them personally of what had happened and to solicit support. He received rapturous support from the junior officers and other ranks at every military unit that he visited on 4th June 1979.

While all this was going on, the coup-makers had quickly set in motion a blitzkrieg involving the arrest of all senior officers, i.e. all those from rank of major and above; wherever they might be. Most of them happened to be at the main barracks, Burma Camp, where, upon being surprised, they were swiftly arrested, starting from dawn of D-day, 4 June. Especially targeted were the members of the Military Tribunal who were trying Rawlings and his men. All were arrested, badly beaten and placed in custody. In the process of effecting these arrests, the President of the Military Tribunal, Colonel Enninful and his wife, were shot dead. As these arrests of officers continued, there was sporadic fighting between forces loyal to the old régime, and those loyal to the incoming régime. Particularly gallant was the stiff resistance which was put up by the best equipped unit in the Army, the Recce Regiment which had foiled the coup of 15 May 1979 led and organised by Rawlings. However, as the coup had started as a confrontation between officers and non-officers, the outcome was inevitable.

The coup of 15 May led by the charismatic Rawlings was engineered by elements in the Air Force. As it failed to get the anticipated army support especialy from the Recce unit, it was

193

bound to collapse. The 4 June coup was a different proposition. It was engineered from elements in the Army, from the Fifth Battalion of Infantry, responsible for the defence of Accra, and its military installations and camps. It was the same Army Unit which Col Acheampong as Brigade Commander had used of for his coup of 13 January 1972. This time many soldiers in this same battalion had joined the few rebel forces. And the release of Rawlings and his men, apart from injecting a massive dose of psychological strength into the coup, had given the coup-makers air-cover, which proved decisive in the battle. Ultimately, the Recce Regiment and the loyal forces came to be at the mercy of the Air Force, who threatened to bomb them into surrender.

Despite these threats, which unknown to them were empty and ineffectual as the military aircraft were technically not equipped for target bombing, the Recce Regiment and a few soldiers fought to the bitter end, till they surrendered.

While the arrests of officers continued and the pitched fights for the control of the military units went on, Rawlings returned from his visits to the military units in different parts of the country. On hearing of the broadcasts of the Army Commander, he gathered his forces together. They ignored the truce offer from the Army Commander, redeployed their forces and made another violent onslaught on the Radio Station, which was now in the hands of the loyal troops. Meanwhile, the Army Commander despatched armoured cars to the Nima Police Station, about two hundred yards from the Radio Station. He had commandeered a few Police Armoured cars (painted blue), and with a handful of Army Armoured cars (painted camouflage green), had established the Police Station as his command post. He integrated resistance against the coup by walkie-talkie.

At the Police Station, a fierce pitched battle took place between the Army Commander (and his few loyal forces) and the "rebellious" forces. The Army Commander and his forces overwhelmingly outnumbered, were defeated, with Major-General Odartey-Wellington himself dying in battle. By 3 p.m. practically all significant resistance to the coup had ended. There continued to be pockets of resistance at different Army Units, but they all rapidly surrendered, and by late afternoon Rawlings was once more on the air to announce that they were now fully and firmly in control of the country. He appealed fervently to all those soldiers still fighting against his forces to give in, to avoid "further bloodshed", and ensure a quick return to normal life.

Meanwhile there was complete chaos in Accra. Shops of Lebanese and Indians were looted. Homes of many officers were ransacked by soldiers, and some wives were allegedly raped or beaten. As military aircraft swooped over the main markets there was complete riot, melée and anarchy, causing many deaths and injuries.

The signal that it was all over was when in the evening of June 4 1979 the Chief of Defence Staff, Lieutenant-General Joshua Hamidu, came on the air to announce that all the major military centres and installations were in the hands of the revolutionary forces and that, in the interests of peace, and to avoid further bloodshed, all troops should cease fighting immediately. As the Head of State at the time, Lt General Akuffo could not be found, the statement of surrender by his deputy on the military junta officially signalled the end of the military government of General Akuffo. The Supreme Military Council (No 2) had come to an end after only eleven months in office. It had not lived to see the return to civilian rule to which it had made such an enormous contribution.

After taking over the main military and civilian centres of power in the country, the coup-makers, formed a new Armed Forces Revolutionary Council (A.F.R.C.) to replace the S.M.C. The Chairman or leader was Flight-Lieutenant Jerry John Rawlings, with Capt Boakye Djan of the 5th Battalion as his

Deputy and official spokesman for the Council. Also on it were two other officers and six non-officers, including a private. As this new military government was introduced to the nation on radio and television in the night on 5 June 1979, it was evident that the country was going through a traumatic and drastic series of changes never before encountered.

For the first time in the country's history, the military junta contained non-officers as active rulers of the land, and the Police were excluded from the administration of the country. It was clear from the early pronouncements of the new régime that having shed considerable blood to achieve their objectives, they were not going to counter any obstruction or resistance from whatever quarter, and that they were prepared, if necessary, to shoot to kill, in order to carry out their programme. Quickly, it transpired that the coup of 4 June 1979, was not an ordinary coup like the previous ones. This one was a rebellion-mutiny-coup, all rolled into one, which rapidly became transformed into a full-blown revolution, challenging the old order, not only in the Army, but in civil life.

It had started originally with "the aim of cleansing the Armed Forces of corrupt, dishonest officers, and restoring the tarnished image of the Armed Forces"; resulting from the activities of most of the officers who had been seconded into civilian jobs; or those who, although staying behind in barracks, were known inexplicably to have made a lot of money. In fact, according to the D.P.P's statement at the trial of Rawlings, the original aim was to go the Ethiopian way, i.e. a large scale decimation of the whole officer corps, with a few exceptions. And although Rawlings' coup had failed, its aims and objectives were adopted by the succeeding coup in 4 June. In the process of removing and dealing with the officers as planned, the rebellious forces were confronted with the Supreme Military Council (who were all Service Commanders) and with the Head of Police. The rebellion thus became a coup. Having challenged and overthrown the established order in the military set-up, belatedly, the new régime turned its attention to the established order in the civilian set-up, thus starting a full revolution in the country.

As such, in the early statements by the new military régime, it was frequently emphasised that its chief objectives were to identify and punish the officers who had tarnished the image of the Armed Forces by their greed and corruption, to rid the Army of bad elements, and to check corruption generally, especially in the Armed Forces. As the weeks passed, these objectives began to be extended outside the military sphere.

That the country was witnessing a revolution, and not merely a coup, was evidenced by the series of events that quickly succeeded the overthrow of the S.M.C. Needless to say, the Military Tribunal which was trying Rawlings and his men died a rather violent death. Its President actually lost his life. The new régime in numerous statements which were broadcast inter-mittently on the radio and television, asked *all* military officers who had served in the military régime, from January 1972 till the day of the Revolution to report at the nearest Police Station or military barracks to be arrested, or risk the military consequences, being shot on sight. A couple of days after ceaselessly calling for the surrender of these officers, the Armed Forces Revolutionary Council (A.F.R.C.) also asked for those who had served in the first post-coup régime (February 1966-October 1969) to report. To many people it made sense to require those who had served in the just-overthrown military junta, and their "military-civilian" colleagues, to report to be arrested. But it was difficult to comprehend what was behind the request for those who had served in the 1966-69 régime also to report.

Many of those who were requested to report did so. There

was little alternative, anyway. A few lucky ones quickly made a dash for the Ghana-Volta border and safely disappeared. The goddess Fortune smiled even more benignly on a few wanted persons. At the time of the Revolution they were either in Britain or somewhere in Europe on business. Obviously, they were not going to take the next plane home to Ghana to be arrested, beaten and probably shot.

To the honour of the Roman Catholic Church, its Bishop in Accra, His Grace Dr Andoh, assisted by Father Hilary Senoo and the American Father Quechmore, apart from giving spiritual assistance to all the wanted persons who sought refuge in the Cathedral in Accra, did everything humanly possible to protect and help these people, irrespective of their religious affiliations.

Among those arrested in the early days of the Revolution was the former Head of State, General I.K. Acheampong, whose coup of January 1972 had, in the opinion of many intelligent observers, set in the train of events which had culminated in the Revolution. Three other Heads of State, General Fred Akuffo, Gen Ankrah, and General A. Afrifa (the hero of the 1966 coup), were also incarcerated.

Following the successful overthrow of the old régime the borders were closed, all air traffic suspended and the country effectively sealed off from the outside world. This was done to prevent the escape of any one who was wanted by the new régime. In addition to these mass arrests, the régime announced the freezing of the assets of these people, and those of their wives and children, and also of firms and businesses in which they were suspected to have interests. This order meant that none of their bank accounts could be drawn on without the approval of the régime. Nor could their properties, cars, farms, personal effects, be sold, bought or transferred in any way, without the specific approval of the Government.

The régime continued to consolidate its hold on the country, by frequently exposing alleged acts of wrongdoing by the arrested people, their acts of dishonesty, greed, corruption and plundering of the state coffers. In different military units throughout the country, the junior officers and other ranks had, on taking over from their superiors, placed them under arrest, shaved their heads and, in some cases, subjected them to merciless beating, humiliating gymnastic exercises and cruel physical and mental torture.

In some of the regional capitals the Police, following the military example, arrested some of their senior officers on alleged charges of bribery, corruption, maladministration and nepotism. They subjected them to rigorous interrogation and manhandling and, finally, placed them in custody. Indeed, the whole situation was getting out of hand. The new régime appointed a Commission of Enquiry, under the chairmanship of an Army Officer, Capt. Karl Huppenbauer**, to investigate the grievances of the Policemen.

While the régime continued to arrest its enenies, both in the Armed Forces and outside, the local radio and television kept up with an unceasing flow of news items from the Armed Forces Revolutionary Council (A.F.R.C.) about details of the alleged corruption of the arrested Senior Officers. They had been given detailed questionnaires to answer about their lives from birth, through education, career, right up to June 4 1979. Specific details of properties, bank accounts (both local and foreign) cars, farms, personal effects, were all asked for. The forms which they were being asked to fill by their junior colleagues and N.C.O's, were similar to those which they, as members of the military régime, had forced the politicians of the Busia régime to comply with when they took over forcibly on 13 January 1972. Nemesis had indeed caught up with them after only seven years.

It should be recorded that while all these arrests and

investigations were going on, massive demonstrations by market women, students, workers, were periodically taking place in the regional capitals, especially in Accra. They were all in fervent support of the new régime and the Revolution, asking for death penalty without trial for the arrested senior officers, especially the members of the S.M.C., and the erstwhile Head of State, Mr I.K. Acheampong. The public demands for bloodshed were more vociferous from the University students at Legon, Kumasi and Cape Coast. Watching some of these demonstrations in June-July 1979, it was hard to imagine that from the same University campuses in January 1972, other students had put up massive public demonstrations to welcome Acheampong's coup and his "Yentua" policy ("We will not pay!") when he unilaterally and arbitrarily repudiated Ghana's debts to the West and encouraged violent demonstrations against the British and American Embassies. Ironically, this time the student demonstrations were *against* Acheampong and his colleagues. Although the student demonstrations again converged on the British, American and Nigerian Embassies, as had happened in January 1972, this time they went to register their protests against these embassies and their countries for appealing to the new A.F.R.C. to treat Acheampong and his arrested colleagues humanely according to due process of law. There may be a lesson or two for all present and future African politicians to learn from these identical incidents, spanned by a period of seven years.

It should be remembered that the Revolution did not materially affect the election campaign which went on unabated. The candidates and politicians continued to tour the country making more and more speeches promising Welfare benefits, jobs, housing and other assistance to the people. The architect of the coup, now the Spokesman of the A.F.R.C., Capt Boaky Djan, and other members of the new régime, continued to repeat their intention not to interfere in any way with the electoral processes towards a return to civilian rule. They kept scrupulously aloof from partisan politics, allowing the electorate to listen to the promises of the various political parties and decide for themselves. Whatever the political affiliations of the different members of the military régime, collectively as a Government, they kept completely aloof from the hurly-burly of politics and did not interfere in any way. The Revolution and the election campaign went on hand in hand.

Amid their deep involvement in the violent and dramatic convulsions in the Armed Forces, the new régime found time to at least peep into the economic problems of the country. On assuming office, they had requested not only Commissioners (i.e. Ministers) and other top people in the Administration to report at the nearest Police Stations and barracks, but had also ordered all top Civil Servants, Heads of State Enterprises and Corporations, Permanent Secretaries and Directors to report. Now never had this happened in Ghana in any coup. The Civil Servants had always been left out, while the politicians whose speeches they were happily writing only a few days previously went off to prison. This time they were also asked to report, to their great dismay and consternation. The general feeling in the country was that all along the civil servants had been let off too lightly. In the 1966 and the 1972 coups they were not touched, although many people felt that some of the civil servants, like the politicians, should also have been made to face Commissions of Enquiry into their assets. The argument that only politicians were corrupt was beginning to wear thin with many people.

However, after these initial arrests, they were all released except the military officers who had held civilian jobs. The civil servants were allowed to continue in their positions and ordered to take over responsibility for their ministries from their arrested "military-civilian Commissioners". The degree of disinterest and callousness which many of these civil servants showed towards their arrested former political masters was most incredible. Nobody was prepared to risk his own job or arrest, by trying to seek permission from the military adminstration to visit the detained masters. Loyalty suddenly vanished.

After re-assigning the senior civil servants to their Ministries and Departments, the A.F.R.C. embarked on a massive nation-wide programme of dealing with the country's endemic economic problems, within the short time at its disposal. Information centres were set up in the capital and in the main towns to which people were invited to report all cases of profiteering, racketeering, corruption, misuse of state funds, excessive rents, etc. Following the information so received, the régime let loose hundreds of armed troops on the towns and villages to force prices down. Well-known business men were arrested. The managing directors, managers, purchasing officers, directors of state Corporations were all ordered to report. Market women who were selling their goods above the arbitrarily fixed prices ruled by the régime, had their goods confiscated, and sold directly to the public. Warehouses belonging to state or private firms were ordered to be broken into, and the contents sold out at low prices. Particularly targeted were the shops of Lebanese, Syrians and Indians.

Food-sellers and other traders who were caught selling above the Government-stipulated controlled prices, were arrested, and sometimes flogged on the spot, by the military. These actions led to strong condemnation by the religious leaders before they were grudgingly brought to an end, after continued pleas from Flight-Lieutenant Rawlings, Capt Boakye Djan and other members of the régime. Lebanese and other foreign traders who, on secret information, were known to be hoarding goods had their warehouses broken into and the goods sold and put into State chest. The owners of such goods were given the then popular military treatment and deported. Some Ghanaian

202

businessmen equally ended in military custody, without trial.

The prices of food and other consumer items dropped suddenly, in most cases to less than half their pre-Revolution levels. Significantly, the high numbers of Lebanese and Indian traders suddenly dropped, as many hurriedly left the country or went underground. For many of these did not have valid immigration papers for their continued residence in Ghana. To stem the mass exodus of wealthy Ghanaians and foreign businessmen the military junta introduced, in 1979, without any publicity or official announcement, a system whereby all persons wishing to leave the country had first to be screened by the Military Police or Military Intelligence. So quiet and secret was the whole scheme that people who did no know about its operation had to be turned away from the airport, just when they were about to board their planes to fly from the country.

Meanwhile, with the whole country in a state of excitement, fear and agitation, with soldiers going up and down the country forcing food prices, rents and transport fares down, liberally dispensing on the spot corporal punishment to those who were deemed to have disobeyed the junta's decrees or orders, with some soldiers taking the law into their own hands in their offical assignments or private escapades, the country was treated to an unusual spectacle. It was that of the former Head of State, Mr I.K. Acheampong, on 14 June 1979, at a press conference publicised on radio and television adroitly answering questions about his past performance during his rule. He shrugged off responsibility for any wrongdoing by his administration. He blamed it all on his colleagues or the top civil servants and played the innocent, aggrieved party. He disclaimed any assets or possessions locally or abroad, contrary to public knowledge and rumour.

On June 14 and 15 there were various public protests to the A.F.R.C. for allowing the former Head of State to flaunt public feelings by his arrogance and lack of remorse for all the sufferings – economic, social and political – which his six year rule had brought on many families. Significant among these sufferings resulting from the Acheampong régime's activities was the death in 1972 of Mr da Rocha, a younger brother of the well-known Accra barrister, Mr B.J. da Rocha, who was General-Secretary of Dr Busia's party at the time of its overthrow by Acheampong. Following an unsuccessful attempted coup in 1972, Mr da Rocha, who had just been released from prison where he had been taken at the time of the coup, was arrested by the security services, and severely tortured. He died while in the custody of the military. Right up to his overthrow, despite many requests by barrister da Rocha to the Acheampong régime for a full account of his brother's death, Acheampong never instituted an enquiry into the young man's death or punished those who were responsible.

No satisfactory or cogent reasons were given for the death by shooting of a number of University students by agents of the régime, in 1977-78 during the frequent demonstrations by the students against the dictatorship of the Acheampong régime, and its refusal to relinquish power and return the country to civilian rule. To many fair-minded people, it was considered the height of provocation in view of all that had passed under his rule for Acheampong to appear on television and talk and behave as if nothing at all had happened.

Responding to the public protests against Acheampong's T.V. show, the military régime issued a public statement that they had interrogated him privately while in custody, had secretly taped his answers and responses to questions, and were anxious for the whole world to see him perform in public as he had done in private, pushing off responsibility for every alleged misdeed of his régime on his colleagues and accepting no responsibility for anything that went wrong. Indeed, at the Press Conference the only positive responsibility which he had accepted was his well-known Cassanova activities. In answer to a question whether it was true that as Head of State, he had many amorous affairs, he shot back the rhetorical question – "How many of you don't flirt with women other than your wives?" In any case, he did not see how his extra-marital, sexual activities had anything to do with the issue of import licences or his administration of the country.

With rumblings still going on about Acheampong's T.V. performance, the public turned its attention to the election campaign, the constant stream of news on radio and T.V. about arrests of prominent people and the details of the assets of the arrested military officers, as published in the State newspapers, and broadcast by the radio and a television. The mass media, owned and controlled by the State, had suddenly made a dramatic turn. They were violently attacking the Rawlings abortive coup of 15 May 1979, fervently blasting its author and leader. But on June 4, Rawlings succeeded and became the national hero. So the press, radio and television made a dramatic change of gear, and began to praise Rawlings and the Revolution to high heavens. This time the attacks were all directed *against* those *against* Rawlings and not overtly enthusiastic about the Revolution. One of the prominent editors, well-known for his anti-Rawlings writings when the Rawlings coup failed on May 15 1979, literally wet his pants on hearing the news on June 4 1979 that Rawlings was in control of the country. For this careful, fastidious gentleman, the news was too much.

All over Ghana, people in prominent positions were quickly re-thinking their positions. Files were mysteriously disappearing, public speeches were being rewritten, and official statements were being recouched to reflect the new "revolutionary" mood. In many cases, the changes were being made happily and effortlessly by the very people who only a few weeks previously were burning the midnight oil exposing "the greed and irresponsibility" of Rawlings, and casting wild aspersions against all half-castes. Now half-castes were being looked on as saviours of Ghana, the torch-bearers of the Ghana Revolution. That's the way of the world – at least in Ghana!

On June 16th 1975 the new revolutionary government announced on the State Radio that Mr Ignatius Kutu Acheampong, the former Head of State, had been *shot* by a firing squad in the early morning. He had been shot with Brigadier Utuka, the former Commander of the Border Guards. According to the statement they had been tried by a secret military Court at Burma Camp barracks and been found guilty of corruption, misuse of state funds and property, criminal negligence, economic sabotage, etc.

However, the general public feeling was that Acheampong's execution was an act of retributive justice. Significiantly, there was no one to mourn Acheampong's death. Even his best friends, including the big business tycoons and associates, who had benefitted immensely from his largesse, at the expense of the State, did not raise a finger or voice of protest. Indeed, they joined in the general chorus of public condemnation of Acheampong. Nor did any of his mistresses register any public protest over his execution. What puzzled many people was why the former Commander of the Border Guard had been executed with Acheampong. After all, it was argued, he was merely an erstwhile Member of the Military junta before its overthrow, and he could have been no more corrupt than other colleagues of his who were still living.

After seven long years, the Army that Acheampong had used destroyed him. It is still worth recording, that long before his execution, he had a sort of spiritual re-awakening, even to the extent of feeling remorse for some of the things which he had done. He went to his death, aged 48, a brave, resolute man, waving his customary white handkerchief to the very end to the few pressmen, soldiers and bystanders near the firing range in Teshie, near Accra. So ended the life of Ignatius Kutu Acheampong, who, by his treacherous act of January 13 1972, unknowingly and unwittingly, set in motion a train of events which were to culminate on 4 June 1979, with the Ghana Revolution. To the extent that his first move in January 1972 led eventually to the cleansing of the whole Ghana society, his death might not be in vain.

*Flight Lieutenant Jerry John Rawlings was born in 1947 in Ghana of Scottish father and Ghanaian mother. His mother is from the Volta Region of Ghana. He was educated in Accra, and at Ghana's famous, prestigious secondary school, Achimota. From there he joined the Ghana Air Force, where he was well-known and admired as an ace-pilot. He was also much admired as an officer very concerned about his men. He was one of the many officers who did not hold any civilian jobs during the whole period of the military régime (1972-79). His mother, a civil servant, was summarily retired following the abortive coup by her son on 15 May 1979. He is married, with one child who was born on 4 June 1978.

**Karl Huppenbauer, like his friend, Flight-Lieutenant Rawlings, is a half-caste, being of Ghanaian mother and German father. Towards the end of the life of the Rawling's régime, the Huppenbauer Commission's Report was presented to the Government, accepted and published. In it were detailed many instances of dishonesty and corruption against certain Senior Police Officers, with recommendations that certain assets were to be forfeited to the State. Some were further to be prosecuted. Other Officers had a few of their properties confiscated, and were retired immediately from the Police Force.

Chapter 11 – Return to Civilian Rule

After the secret, unannounced "trials" and public execution of Acheampong and Utuka (the former Commander of the Border Guards) and others, the Armed Forces Revolution Council, turned its attention to the civilian population. The revolution which was meant to be *merely* a "house-cleaning exercise in the Armed Forces", in order to rid it of corrupt and bad elements and "restore its tarnished image" now spread its wings to engulf the civilians also. By July 1979, the public information centres to which the public were invited to report all known or suspected crimes against the state were actively busy. After the long period of Acheampong's government there were many people who had personal vendettas to settle with a number of military officers. As such, any person who was known to have been formerly a friend of the overthrown Acheampong-Akuffo régime, or who had benefitted considerably from the régime (through the receipt of import licences or state loans or business assistance) was at risk. In such a situation, many unscrupulous people took the advantage to report others who they believed to be a threat to their own promotion prospects, or were indebted to them, or were their business or trade competitors, or were even amorous rivals. Cases were also known of some people getting their soldier friends to pursue debts on their behalf.

The mass arrests of civilians, especially the wealthier ones, which resulted from the extension of the ambit of the revolution caused considerable fear and uncertainty in the civilian population, which had until then accepted that the revolution was limited to only the Armed Forces. Nobody felt safe. Nobody

209

knew for certain when and where the axe might fall next. Coupled with these arrests – particularly of big traders, contractors, businessmen and women – was the habit of certain soldiers beating on the spot people who they had arrested for having broken any of the numerous decrees against hoarding of goods, over-pricing, profiteering, or refusal to sell. In fact, the situation was getting so out of control that the religious bodies (especially the Council of Churches) and the Bar Association had to plead with the revolutionary council to ensure that these public beatings, especially of women, were stopped. Even Rawlings himself, on a few occasions, spoke publicly against the absurd cases of people who had been arrested or beaten for having hoarded goods. Upon proper examination it sometimes turned out to be only six tins of sardines or a dozen tins of milk.

It was in this atmosphere of near-anarchy, fear and confusion that the country to its shock and utter amazement learnt on the State radio that six senior military officers, including two heads of state, had been shot by firing squad after secret "trials" by the People's Court set up by the revolutionary council. All those executed were alleged to have committed various offences against the State. They were all members of the Acheampong-Akuffo military Council (S.M.C.I. and 2), except General A.A. Afrifa, who had been Head of State, but had become a road-haulage contractor by 1970. Indeed, at the time of his execution, he had already been cleared by the Sowah Committee, which had been set up to investigate all past military officers or civilians who had held positions in previous régimes and who wanted to re-enter politics or hold state office. He had stood for election in his home town, Ashanti Mampong, as a candidate of the United National Convention (U.N.C.) and had won a parliamentary seat by a large majority. His death was simply inexplicable to many people. But to many others who had been direct or indirect victims of the Kotoka-Afrifa coup of February

1966, his execution was welcomed.

The death by firing squad of the second batch of military officers brought a tremendous re-awakening in the country. A few people who had publicly hailed the onset of the revolution were beginning to talk and grumble, after these executions. Privately, the public criticisms of the new régime's methods and actions were growing rapidly. The Council of Churches protested strongly and openly against the secret trials and executions and called for their *immediate* stop. Particularly vociferous and defiant were the leaders of the Roman Catholic Church, especially Archbishop Kodwo Amissah, Bishop Andoh, and Father Senoo. They not only publicly and unreservedly challenged the gross injustice in these secret trials and executions, but went out of their way, *at immense risk to their own lives, to plead personally and frequently with Rawlings and his colleagues to stop further executions and bring to open trial all the arrested people.* Apart from praying for all those in trouble, the leaders of the Roman Catholic church, by their timely, defiant and persistent intervention with the revolutionary government, saved the lives of a further 53 persons scheduled for execution.

The Bar Association also pleaded with the Armed Forces Revolutionary Council to stop secret trials and executions and bring all those arrested to open trial by due processes of law. At a period of mass-hysteria and excitement, when most of the public were openly clamouring for more deaths and executions of so-called enemies of the State, plunderers of the State, saboteurs, subvertionists, traitors; at a time when the University Students were jubilantly demonstrating with: "Let the Blood Flow" as their slogan; at a time when everybody was in fear of his own life, the bold and courageous stand which was taken by Miss Elizabeth Ohene (acting) editor of the country's largest circulation paper, the *"Daily Graphic"*, against secret Kangaroo trials and public executions would remain immemorable in the country's history. Despite the immense risk to her career and life, this young lady, accepting at its face value the often repeated statement of the revolutionaries that the press was free, wrote a series of powerful, trenchant editorials passionately pleading for moderation by the régime, and for the need to subject all those arrested to the due process of law. She also had the immense courage to remind the members of the new junta and their advisors and friends that the people wildly acclaiming them and their actions were the same ones who had welcomed Acheampong's triumph in January 1972, Acheampong's fall in July 1978, Akuffo's triumph in July 1978, and his execution in June 1979. The logic of her clearly reasoned editorials was obvious.

For those students demonstrating in front of the Nigerian, British and American Embassies asking for more "blood to flow", and for all those millions of men and women in the country without any sense of history, who naively thought that what was happening to others could never happen to them, Miss Ohene aptly reminded them of what might happen with the famous quotation from Paster Niemmoller.

A prominent military officer whose life was in dire danger at the time told me that he was in tears as he read that editorial. The stand and activities of this young, noble lady, at a time when many prominent people had lost their nerves or heads, would stand as a lasting tribute to Ghanaian women, and the Ghanaian journalistic profession. The public animosity and hatred which she called upon herself were such that Rawlings himself had to step in to save her. At a public meeting in Accra with the students who were demanding her dismissal and trial as a traitor and subversionist, Rawlings boldly and publicly told the students and the public to "leave the lady alone to do her work". The ironic situation had thus been reached where Rawlings, having set in motion a whole train of events by his original programme of "going the Ethiopian way" to clean the country, was compelled, again and again, to put a damper on the activities of some of his most fervent supporters – the students.

The *Echo,* a privately-owned Sunday paper, the *Statesman* and *Punch,* also privately-owned, made some pleas for moderation and for the people whose lives were in danger.

Also deserving of praise were the protests from many parts of the world, especially from Britain, the U.S. and Nigeria, for an end to the executions and the urgent need to accord all the people who had been arrested due process of law. These pleas led to further student demonstrations against the embassies of these countries and the outpouring of vitriolic letters about them in the local papers. The irony of the whole situation is that these diplomatic pleas came mostly from countries whose embassies had been the victims of student and other public demonstrations during the era of Acheampong.

The sustained pleas from foreign countries, the cutting of Ghana's oil supply from Nigeria (on repayment and technical-refinery problems) all cumulatively bore fruit. Rawlings announced on radio and television an end to the public executions and stated that, in future, all those convicted by the People's Courts would be sentenced to periods of hard labour on penal farms. The announcement dramatically brought down the emotional barometer in many households. At the rate at which the executions were taking place it was fair to surmise that practically every town would have made a sacrifice in one form or another.

The General Elections took place without much incident on June 18th 1979. The turn-out was low due probably to the general wait-and-see attitude of the rural people (who constitute about 75 per cent of the population). The Armed Forces Revolutionary Council (A.F.R.C.) kept its undertaking given when it assumed office that it would not in anyway interfere with the elections or the results. The election showed a clear, narrow victory for the People's National Party (P.N.P.), political inheritors of the old Convention People's Party. The main opposition party became the Popular Front Party, the successor party of Dr Busia's Progress Party. Subsequently, the Presidential Election run-off was held on July 9th 1979, between the two candidates with the first two highest votes. In this contest between Dr Hilla Limman of the P.N.P. and Mr Victor Owusu of the P.F.P., by an informal or formal alliance, all the major political parties joined together against the P.F.P. candidate.

The low turn-out had also been caused by the failure of many voters to register during the Acheampong régime when the registration was effected for the purposes of the Union Government referendum on 30 March 1978. Many of those strongly opposed to the whole concept of Union Government refused to register to participate in a fraudulent election whose results were a foregone conclusion. By the demands of the prevailing political climate, most of these people were supporters of the Popular Front Party.

A careful study of the voting procedures at a few polling booths clearly demonstrates that the elections were fair and free. Although there were a very few, isolated instances of electoral malpractices and double-voting, they constituted such a minute fraction of the whole voting process as not to have materially affected the overall results. In any case, such election offences were not limited to any particular political group, and, therefore, presumably would cancel out in effect. On the other hand, a misinterpretation of the registration and voting laws must have materially affected the electoral chances of the P.F.P. in a few constituencies, especially those with considerable numbers of immigrants. This was due to certain political action which the

Progress Party Government of Dr Busia took in 1979, when it properly enforced the new immigration laws decreed by its predecessor. By so acting, many immigrants without valid immigration documents had to leave the country. But in all the cities and towns sizeable pockets of immigrants remained behind. Many of these were not citizens of Ghana, by law, and therefore were not entitled to vote. However, in the registration effected under Acheampong they had all been allowed to register. For Acheampong, being anti-Busia, found a natural ally in these immigrants, some of whose friends or relatives had left the country. The Progress Party Government had earned the nickname of "the anti-alien party", during its period of office.

Between the two presidential candidates, Dr Limann (for the PNP) and Mr Victor Owusu, (for the PFP), the former had the advantage that very little was known about him and thus he could present a fresh image. The very fact that Mr Victor Owusu had held a number of very senior prominent positions since 1966, albeit admirably well, was held against him for being one of "the same old faces". The public wanted a major, fresh change. In that sense, Limann was the man of the day. Apart from the fact that he had been in the foreign service, which had thus kept him out of the hurly-burly of Ghana politics, very little else was known about him.

It has been postulated that Victor Owusu lost because there was a deep, nation-wide anti-Ashanti feeling throughout the country. The argument was that two Heads of State, Afrifa and Acheampong, came from Ashanti, and that it was high time for a non-Ashanti to become a Head of State. To some extent, this view is correct, especially in the southern and northern sections of the country. But oddly enough even in Ashanti, where Victor Owusu hails from, his opponent did rather well.

In terms of electoral programmes, the two major political parties promised the electorate very identical benefits – more schools, hospitals, food, subsidized housing, water supply, more jobs. Admittedly the language and rhetoric of the victorious party was more to the left of centre, while the Popular Front Party, would be accurately described a centre party, rather like Britain's Liberal Party. There were no major identifiable differences between both parties. Even the P.N.P. had avoided the word *Socialism* in its manifesto, presumably aware of the public's idea of socialism as practised by its predecessor-party, the C.P.P.

Finally, two other factors must be stated for probably accounting for the P.N.P. victory. Firstly, having been in the political doldrums for about thirteen years (1966-1979) its members were better motivated towards working for victory and a livelihood. It was a question of a struggle for existence. Secondly, they had far more effective grass-roots contacts and support than the P.F.P.

Both parties had their martyrs. The photographs of Dr Nkrumah who had died in exile in 1972 in Guinea, were extensively used in the election campaign by the PNP. Equally, the P.F.P. made full use of the photographs of Dr Busia, who had died in exile in September 1978 in Britain.

What then was the effect of the general elections on the revolution which was then going on? It is one of the most fascinating aspects of Ghana politics that a revolution and an election could go on simultaneously without one interfering with the other. Before the elections, the new revolutionary régime had given the undertaking at a press conference that the "house-clearing" exercise which they had embarked on in the Armed Forces would take about three or four months to complete; and that after that period they would readily hand over to the party which had won the election, according to the new Constitution. October 1 1979 was fixed as the day for the return to civilian rule. A joint P.N.P. – A.F.R.C. committee was then set up to draw the programme for the return to civilian rule.

As the day for the return to civilian rule approached, the military régime, in a haste, extended its house-clearing exercise to more and more civilian organisations. For the first time in Ghana's history, institutions which had been held sacrosanct after every coup were now attacked. They included Senior civil servants, heads, deputy heads and managers of state enterprises and corporations, private Ghanaian and non-Ghanaian business people and retired Army officers. In short, the régime using the radio was calling regularly people from various walks of life to report to the main barracks in Accra, or sometimes to the nearest barracks. The "revolutionary news" which suddenly became a most disturbing feature of the revolution, towards September 1979 heightened tension in the country. Nobody knew for certain whether his name would be called next, when colleagues and friends and relatives, prominent and not so prominent, were all being called to report or face the military consequences, or "have themselves to blame", as the announcements often ended.

Naturally, in this highly charged atmosphere the planes leaving the country were packed, despite the screening process introduced by the military to check the mass exodus. A few fortunate persons on hearing their names called on the state radio found it more prudent to head for the neighbouring African states, Togo, Ivory Coast or Upper Volta, by car or on foot, while others headed for Britain. In a situation where three Heads of State had lost their lives, properties and assets, and numerous others (mostly senior military officers and a few civilians) were being secretly sentenced to heavy terms of imprisonment from ten to fifty years, it was wise to leave one's assets and funds behind and save one's life! As the radio orders for specified persons to report were preceded by statements that the revolutionary régime had forfeited all their assets, anyway, it really did not make any material difference whether one was

217

there or not to oversee them.

With the elections over and preparations going ahead for the installation of the new civilian government, the major question now was how the "house cleaning" exercise started by Rawlings and his colleagues could be carried on after the handing over date. All the leaders of the political parties had undertaken to complete the house cleaning exercise if they won. Now, with the P.N.P. victorious, its leader Dr Limann re-stated this undertaking. For it was evident that without this commitment, the military would have refused to hand over. Some of them felt that the politicians could not be trusted to continue the exercise with gusto and determination and that somewhere on the line there would be inexplicable trial delays, releases and discharges of persons that they felt were guilty of serious anti-state crimes and activities. The whole hysterical atmosphere in the country was such that any political leader failing to give the undertaking to continue the exercise would have been looked upon by the public as condoning and conniving at bribery and corruption, misappropriation of state funds and misuse of state property.

In fact during the election, one minor political party, the Social Democratic Party, had gone to the extent of requesting a postponement of the elections, and therefore the date for a return to civilian rule. Needless to say, the major parties, heavily geared for the elections, had refused to countenance this suggestion. And so did the military régime for its own reasons.

Until a fortnight before the handing over, there were still rumblings in the Army, against the handing over on the grounds that the house cleaning exercise had just got on the way, and was not yet completed. But the military junta, headed by Flight Lieutenant Rawlings, felt that as they had given their firm word to hand over to a duly elected civilian government under the new Constitution, they would not go back on that promise. This desire on the part of the military régime to keep to the deadline for a return to civilian rule by October 1 1979, or earlier if possible, would explain the over-hasty and tense orders on the State Radio for so many people to report at the designated military barracks.

The political leaders, and especially the new President-elect, Dr Hilla Limann, having given the undertaking to continue with the house cleaning exercise, had a major dilemma to deal with. The People's Courts, whose location, personnel and proceedings were all secret, had, apart from the trial and execution of the eight senior officers, imposed draconian periods of penal hard labour on several senior officers and a few civilians. In addition to these sentences, their assets, properties, funds, and those of their wives and children had been confiscated by the State. Moreover, they had in most cases, been badly beaten and humiliated.

Under the new Constitution human rights and free access, without hindrance, to the Courts, are provided for. Indeed the 1979 post-revolutionary Constitution was a great improvement on the 1969 Constitution. From the experience of the past, specific entrenched clauses had been incorporated to guard against one-party state, dictatorship, arbitrary rule, tyranny etc. It therefore meant that those arrested and detained persons still alive by the handing over date could legally apply to the civilian Courts for a redress of their cases. This was a constitutional right of theirs which could not be denied. On the other hand, the military junta before handing over had insisted on it being incorporated in the new Constitution that no future Government could reverse or alter any of the sentences imposed by the Armed Forces Revolutionary Council. As such, while the cause of justice demanded that these sentences be reviewable by the civilian courts, under the new civilian régime, any such action would technically amount to a breach of the Constitution by the new civilian administration of Dr Limann.

Meanwhile, the joint A.F.R.C./P.N.P. Commission planning the details of the programme for the return to civilian rule had submitted its report and advised that the return to civilian rule could take place on 24 September 1979, instead of 1 October. Nigeria, the largest and richest African State, was having its ceremony of return to civilian rule on 1 October 1979, and it would obviously not have been appropriate for the two ceremonies to take place the same day in the two neigh-bouring West African States. The necessary ceremonial preparations were made, with invitations being sent to all friendly countries.

On 24 September 1979, at about 11 a.m. at a most impressive and colourful ceremony, with the bunting and flags flying in brilliant sunshine, Flight-Lieutenant Jerry John Rawlings, the ace pilot, whose desire to go the "Ethiopian Way" had started the whole revolution in Ghana, handed over the reins of government to the newly elected President of Ghana's Third Republic, Dr Hilla Limman, in Parliament House, at Accra. The ceremony brought to an end four months of short, sharp military rule, which had indeed revolutionised the whole country. Many countries were represented at the ceremony by their Ministers or Ambassadors. President Sekou Toure of Guinea was there in person to see power transferred to the successor party of his good friend, the late Dr Nkrumah.

The speech which Rawlings made on this historic moment, his last as a Head of State and that of Dr Limman are worth studying in full. For they give an indication of the trends of the unfinished Ghana Revolution and the nature of the forces which might determine the course of political events in the country in the foreseeable future.

After the handing over ceremony, Jerry Rawlings, his deputy Capt Boakye Djan, and the rest of the Military junta, went to rejoin their units at a major military parade in Black Star Square, in Accra. Watching the persons who only a few minutes ago were virtual dictators of the country rejoin their units and march past in allegiance to the new Head of State, President Hilla Limman, was a very memorable occasion. It was something more than that, for it marked the complete and unconditional transfer of power by the military to the freely elected representatives of the sovereign people of Ghana. As the ceremony ended and the fleet of official cars disappeared into history and the sound of the soldiers marching receded, many Ghanaians sighed with relief. They were overjoyed that the country had returned to civilian rule, and hoped fervently that the 24 September 1979 ceremony would be the last of its kind in the country's history. For whatever may be the political differences which they may harbour one thing all Ghanaians are agreed upon – that never again should the military rule the nation. *Never again, never again*, was the constant refrain.

Epilogue

Yet, with all the excitement and sighs of relief, there was an uneasy feeling in the air. For precisely ten years before, a similar handing-over ceremony had been held in the same city at the same venues – Parliament (the State House) and Black Star Square. It was then hoped in October 1969 that *never again* should the military rule the nation. There were the usual self-congratulations, expert prognosis and commentaries on the body politic, and everything seemed beautiful. Twenty seven months later an obscure, unknown Lieutenant-Colonel and a handful of colleagues, launched the country into an unnecessary, un-warranted coup d'etat whose ramifications and reverberations were to precipitate, over a period of seven years, the Ghana Revolution. Although legally the Ghana Revolution lasted for four months the traumatic changes which it made in Ghanaian society were such that the country would never be the same again.

The Revolution was unfinished, in that legally it had to terminate on 24 September 1979, but by then it had set in motion a train of events which would continue to affect the society for many years to come. Never before in the history of the country had a President or Head of State been shot or publicly executed. Besides, senior civil servants, directors, and managers of State Corporations and institutions, businessmen and women, retail trade, import trade, local transport, and food distribution had all been affected. And to that extent the 4 June 1979 coup was not merely a coup, but something far more fundamental. What had started at dawn on that day as an army rebellion, by a few units, in the 5th Battalion of Infantry, quickly metamorphosed into a coup, which rapidly matured into a revolution. But for the timely intervention of Capt Boakye Djan and Flight Lieutenant Rawlings the whole revolution would have ended in anarchy and a complete and prolonged break-down in law and order. For many of the soldiers in the heydays of the revolution were determined to kill all officers, on the basis of Rawlings' "Ethiopian Way" programme. On a few occasions during the four months period, it was the other ranks who were armed, and being numerically superior, ruled the officers. That the explosive situation was quickly brought under control and contained within fair limits must be to the credit of these two officers especially. At the initial stages of the revolution in June-July 1979, when the University Students and the public at large were avidly and publicly demanding that more blood should flow, with the other ranks bent on settling old scores with particular officers, the Armed Forces Revolutionary Council stood up firmly against their own forces and supporters, and said loudly and clearly "Enough is Enough".

With the installation of a new freely-elected, democratic civilian Government under the new Constitution, it was the moral and constitutional duty of all Ghanaians and friends of Ghana to support the new Government. Admittedly, not all people would like the P.N.P. Government. Some would have preferred the Popular Front Party or the Social Democratic Party or the United National Convention to have won. But the fact still remains that the sovereign people of Ghana, given a free opportunity to choose their own government, chose the P.N.P. administration.Whether the margin of victory was narrow or the turnout poor is really irrelevant at that stage in the proceedings. What was important for the country as a whole was that the new Administration having been duly installed, under the new Constitution should be given all the support that it is constitutionally entitled to, so that it could run its normal constitutional period of office of four years. That, in my opinion would be political maturity, and a sign of progress. At the end of that period the people of Ghana would know whether they had made the right decisions, or not. However, support for the Government cannot and should not be uncritical and unconditional. That would be a licence for unbridled rule. The public support for the Government should be on the condition that the Government itself obeys and respects the spirit and letter of the constitution, the ultimate law of the land.

It is conventional for most modern nations to have had one major revolution in their history. The English had theirs in 1688-89. The Americans in 1776, the Russians in 1917, the French in 1789, the Chinese in 1949. In each case, it has been one and only one Revolution, to date. Let us hope and trust that Ghana's Revolution of June 1979 was its first and last. And in connection with the June 1979 events we are reminded of Carlyle: "Sire", answered Liancourt, "it is not a revolt, it is a revolution".

APPENDIX I

Dates of Important Events since Independence

1957 Independence

1960 Ghana becomes a republic after a referendum

1964 One-party state established

1966 First military coup d'etat, resulting in Nkrumah's fall

1967 Abortive military coup, resulting in first public execution of the officers involved.

1969 First post-coup general election resulting in the formation of the Busia Government.

1972 Second military coup, resulting in the formation of the National Redemption Council Government under Col I.K. Acheampong.

1972 Abortive coup against Acheampong's régime, resulting in the death in military custody of Mr da Rocha, younger brother of the General Secretary of the Progress Party Government. Death of Dr Nkrumah in Guinea.

1973 Release of political detainees (including the author) from prison by the Acheampong régime.

1976 National Redemption Council replaced by Supreme Military Council (1) as the new Government, still under Acheampong.

1977 "Union Government" concept floated by Acheampong.

1978 Demonstrations, strikes against "Union Government", and the régime. Referendum is held and régime announces that there was YES for Union Governemtn. Many people suspect the referendum as rigged, and, especially the professional bodies, challenge the régime, with more strikes. Acheampong removed in a palace coup by his deputy and colleagues, and imprisoned in 1978. Replaced by his deputy General Akuffo.

1979 May – Rawlings makes an abortive coup.

June – Capt. Boakye Djan organises and leads a successful coup, which effects the release of Ft Lt Jerry J. Rawlings. Coup matures into a Revolution led by Rawlings, with several senior military officers, and ex-Presidents publicly executed by firing squad. General Elections held, resulting in victory of P.N.P.

July – Presidential elections, resulting in the election of Dr Limman as first President of the Third Republic.

September – Handing over of power from Rawlings régime to President Limman and his Administration.

December – Rawlings and his appointees as service commanders all retired from the Armed Forces.

APPENDIX II

Whether the Ghanain Revolution of 1979 was justified or not, will continue to be debated for a long time. However, if ever there was a Government whose words and deeds, convicted and sentenced itself, then the military régime in Ghana, pre 1979, was a good example.

For in a country where heavy sentences are passed by the courts for the theft of a chicken, it was most incomprehensible to put it mildly, for the Akuffo régime to have issued a long and damning public document, charging the previous Head of State, with numerous, heinous crimes, and then given him the sentence of *releasing* him from custody and only limiting him to a leisurely confinement to his village!

The immorality of the régime's action, let alone its gross lack of imagination, was plain for all to see. Little wonder that the handling of the problem of the deposed Head of State, who had been removed from office in July 1978, by the Akuffo régime, helped to fuel the forces culminating in the Revolution of 1979.

The following is the full text of the damning and problematic decree, which in an effort to solve the Acheampong Question, created even more questions and problems. It is for readers to decide whether the punishment meted out in the Acheampong case fitted the alleged crimes.

ARMED FORCES (MISCELLANEOUS PROVISIONS) DECREE, 1979

Whereas on the morning of 13th January, 1972 Ignatius Kutu Acheampong as an Acting Colonel in command of the 1st Infantry Brigade Group announced to the whole world on Radio Ghana that the Ghana Armed Forces and the Police had overthrown the lawfully constituted Government of the Second Republic of Ghana and suspended the 1969 Constitution and in justifying that action, promised to redeem the "shattered" economy of Ghana and to restore individual liberties and the unity of the nation;

And whereas in the course of six and half years in office as Head of State, he by selfish, careless and irresponsible acts, plunged the country into the most deplorable state of economic disrepair and national apathy and brought the Armed Forces into disrepute and created a breach between its members and the general public and by his actions and omissions while in office as Head of State not only did he grievously aggravate the state of the economy but also systematically subverted both national unity and the command structure and discipline of the Armed Forces;

And whereas the Supreme Military Council is satisfied that among the list of economic, administrative and other misconduct which he committed against the State and people of Ghana during his term of office were included the following in the economic sphere:-

(a) personally interfering in the economic and financial management of the nation, thereby creating grave distortions in properly planned programmes,

(b) indiscriminate issue outside the officially recognised machinery of import licences to favourites and close associates,

(c) awarding contracts to incompetent favourites,

(d) interfering in the normal operations of the Bank of Ghana including causing the over-printing and over-issue of cedi notes,

(e) taking dubious foreign loans to the detriment of the State,

(f) personally granting underserved concessions to favourite business houses in contravention of existing government policy and regulation.

And whereas in the political and administrative sphere he in furtherance of his inordinate ambition for power, manipulated and vested all executive power in his person to his own advantage, thereby enabling him to disregard with impunity the principles of collective responsibility of colleagues in the National Redemption.

Council and the Supreme Military Council and by that means he took and reversed several important decisions in the name of the National Redemption Council and the Supreme Military Council without prior consultation with his colleagues;

And whereas similarly, against the good judgement of his colleagues he employed at State expense the services of numerous unofficial personal advisers and aides of dubious competence, character and intention who only sought their own good in government to the detriment of the nation;

And whereas through a systematic use of cunning and subtle interference he brought the Armed Forces to the brink of disintegration and showered generous favours on certain officers and men known to be closely associated with him to the disadvantage and annoyance of other officers of merit and of the rank and file which acts contributed materially to the breakdown of discipline in the Armed Forces;

And whereas he appointed into sensitive jobs certain favourite serving and retired officers of questionable competence whose performance badly tarnished the image of the Armed Forces in the eyes of the public;

And whereas in addition to all these grave acts of misconduct he was guilty of the most scandalous conduct involving complete display of moral turpitude unbecoming of an officer and a gentleman, even more particularly of a Head of State;

And whereas he adopted the habit of maintaining spurious religious advisers with substantial foreign exchange from the nation's scarce resources and used their advice as subterfuge for doing wrong to the detriment of the nation;

And whereas in view of these acts which have resulted in serious prejudice to the State and the people and the Armed Forces of Ghana, the Supreme Military Council as the Government and as constituted by the Commander-in-Chief, the Chief of Defence Staff and all the Service Commanders of the Armed Forces of Ghana have accordingly decided to divest Ignatius Kutu Acheampong of all the honours acquired by him during his tenure of office.

Now, THEREFORE, BE IT ENACTED by the Supreme Military Council as follows:-

1. With effect from the commencement of this Decree Ignauius Kutu Acheampong shall be deemed to have been divested of every military rank or title previously held or possessed by him.

2. The said Ignatius Kutu Acheampong shall, with effect from the said date be deemed to have been divested of all State honours whether civil, military or otherwise previously acquired by him.

3. The said Ignatius Kutu Acheampong shall, from the said

date be deemed to have been deprived of all retirement benefits and awards conferred on him or for which he would otherwise have been eligible in respect of his service as a member of the Armed Forces of Ghana and otherwise.

4. (1) The said Ignatius Kutu Acheampong shall, subject to the provisions of this section, be released forthwith from preventive custordy but shall after the commencement of this Decree reside in his village, that is to say, Trabuom in the Ashanti Region of Ghana.

(2) Notwithstanding anything in subsection (1) of this section the said Ignatius Kutu Acheampong shall be taken in the custody of a police officer or a member of the Armed Forces to Trabuom and there released.

(3) Whenever the said Ignatius Kutu Acheampong leaves Trabuom without the permission of the Supreme Military Council or any person authorised by that Council –

(a) he shall be guilty of an offence and liable upon summary conviction to a term of imprisonment not exceeding five years without the option of a fine;

(b) any police officer or member of the Armed Forces may arrest and detain him, using such force as may be necessary and reasonable for the purpose of taking him to Trabuom.

5. (1) The said Ignatius Kutu Acheampong shall not, unless while he is under lawfulo custody, enter any military barracks, camp, establishment or installation whatsoever.

(2) Contravention of subsection (1) of this section shall be punishable on summary conviction by a term of imprisonment not exceeding five years without the option of a fine.

6. This Decree shall have effect notwithstanding the provisions of the Armed Forces Act, 1961 (Act 105) and any regulations made thereunder.

7. The Preventive Custody (No 42) Order, 1978 (E.I.150) is

hereby revoked.

8. This Decree shall come into force on the 1st day of May, 1979.

Made this 1st day of May, 1979.

GENERAL F.W.K. AKUFFO
Chairman of the Supreme Military Council

LT-GENERAL JOSHUA HAMIDU
Chief of Defence Staff

B.S.K. KWAKYE, ESQ
nspector-General of Police

MAJOR-GENERAL N.A.ODARTEY-WELLINGTON
Army Commander

REAR-ADMIRAL J.K. AMEDUME
Navy Commander

AIR VICE-MARSHAL G.Y. BOAKYE
Air Force Commander

MAJOR-GENERAL K. OSEI BOATENG
Border Guard Commander

Date of *Gazette* notification: 4th May, 1979